**WITHDRAWN
UTSA Libraries**

WORLD AFFAIRS
National and International Viewpoints

WORLD AFFAIRS
National and International Viewpoints

The titles in this collection were selected
from the Council on Foreign Relations' publication:
The Foreign Affairs 50-Year Bibliography

Advisory Editor
RONALD STEEL

ECONOMIC PLANNING
AND
INTERNATIONAL ORDER

BY
LIONEL ROBBINS

Preface by Lionel Robbins

ARNO PRESS
A NEW YORK TIMES COMPANY
New York • 1972

Reprint Edition 1972 by Arno Press Inc.

Reprinted by permission of Macmillan and Co., Ltd.

Reprinted from a copy in The Newark Public Library

World Affairs: National and International Viewpoints
ISBN for complete set: 0-405-04560-3
See last pages of this volume for titles.

Manufactured in the United States of America

Library of Congress Cataloging in Publication Data

Robbins, Lionel Charles Robbins, Baron, 1898-
　Economic planning and international order.

　(World affairs: national and international viewpoints)
　Reprint of the 1937 ed.
　Bibliography: p.
　1. Economic policy.　2. Competition, International.
3. International cooperation.　I. Title.　II. Series.
HD82.R6　1972　　　　330　　　72-4294
ISBN 0-405-04586-7

LIBRARY
University of Texas
At San Antonio

PREFACE

In authorising a republication of this work, written more than 35 years ago, I should like it to be read in the light of the account of its origin and the criticism of its contents which appear in my *Autobiography of an Economist,* published in 1971.

In that work, after relating my particular experiences in the great controversy over free trade and protection which took place in Great Britain in the early thirties, I write that, reflecting on this controversy and the current developments, "I decided upon an entirely new approach to the problem. The vogue of tariffs was clearly part of a wider tendency to interference by national states with the international division of labour. The current fashion indeed was all for national plans of one sort or another, whose common characteristic was diversion of resources from the pattern they would have assumed under the incentives of the forces of the market, a process which besides involving a progressive spilling of wealth, either actually or potentially, meant also the possible creation of political frictions on a scale eventually dangerous to peace. The traditional case for liberalism in the sphere of international economic relations had relied chiefly upon national self-interest, leaving the international case to emerge inferentially. Why should I not reverse the procedure and tackle the international interest directly? This, it seemed to me, would have two advantages. Analytically it permitted considerable simplification. From the national point of view the analysis of obstacles to trade had to take account of exceptions such as the possible short-run advantages of influences on the terms of the bargain — practically unimportant as in the long run these were likely to be — and this, . . . had a cramping effect on exposition. From the international point of view these complications assumed a far smaller position in the perspective: the contraction of trade and the misallocation of resources stood out far more clearly and the possible advantages of unilateral national action could be compared with the national interest in international cooperation. At the same time, an approach from this point of view would surely have some relevance to that sense of the solidarity of the civilised tradition and unease at the inappropriateness of the anarchic political organisation of the world which, although not by any means dominant, was one of the more valuable features of the surviving liberal tradition of the West.

"Accordingly, in 1935, when William Rappard, one of the truly great men of the inter-war period, invited me to lecture at his Geneva Institute, I took this as my theme and subsequently elaborated what I had said into a book which I called *Economic Planning and International Order* . . . .

"Unlike *The Great Depression,* this is not a work I should now wish not to have written. On the plane on which it elects to move, although naturally there are some things I should now put somewhat differently, I still stand by most of the arguments there put forward. I have nothing to retract in the survey of the conflicts of interest created by economic nationalism. I still stand firmly on the exhibition of the conflict between the allocative principle and what I called 'the *the*-industry fallacy'. I would not wish to alter the analysis of the probable results of compulsory equalization of rates of pay between areas where productivity rates are not equal. The allocative and incentive difficulties of collectivism without effective markets seem to me to have been overwhelmingly demonstrated in recent history, as have the dangers to personal freedom and a democratic way of life. As for the general arguments for federalism as a remedy for international anarchy and the general conception of liberalism as a framework of law and order designed to harmonise individual and group initiative, I would not wish to subtract anything, though, needless to say, there is much that could be added. Unlikely though its realisation may be, I am not ashamed of this chapter as a statement of my Utopia and I am a little proud to have revived the arguments of *The Federalist* rather earlier than elsewhere.

"Nevertheless, the book as a whole seems now to me to suffer from two not inconsiderable deficiencies. First comes one which clearly springs from the inadequacy of my views at that time of macro-economic problems. I do not abate one jot my strictures on the contemporary restrictionism and economic nationalism. But I think I should have recognised more explicitly the fact that some at least of such manifestations were almost compulsive reactions, ill conceived no doubt, to the prevalent pressures of general deflation. There is not sufficient recognition of the need for the allocative principle to be realised in a *milieu* of reasonably brisk utilization of resources. And in the chapter on international money, while there is much which I think is true and deserves continually to be kept in mind, there is still insufficient recognition of the need for an international system which is so planned as to avoid the evils of both deflation and inflation. There is admission of the inadequacy of our knowledge in this connection. But it is not stated, as I should now wish it to be stated, that, in the absence of such arrangements, no power on earth will prevent the authorities of national states from having their own monetary policies which, as often as not, are likely to lead to all the confusions and frustrations set forth in this chapter.

"Secondly, while not retracting anything said in favour of the federal principle as an instrument of international order, I am clear now that there is a substantial lack of realism about the conceptions of the areas of its applicability. The strong apprehensions with which I wrote concerning the dangers of peace and order of the anarchy of relations between the Western Powers led me incautiously to use modes of expression which implied that the supranational arrangements, so desperately needed in that area, were as easily conceivable and as immediately desirable for the world as a whole. But this is obviously not true for our generation. Few inhabitants of Europe or America would wish to have their destinies decided by a world federal authority elected on a one-man, one-vote basis. As I was to say later on in a paper on 'Liberalism and the International Problem' which, better than anything I have written, embodies my present views on this problem, 'It is possible that as the years go on, the intense proselytizing zeal of the totalitarian powers may burn itself out and the intelligent youth, bored with the ancient slogans, may come to see less of an enemy in the ideals of the free society, in which case, more comprehensive unions might be hoped for. But that time is not yet. As things are, men would fight not to join such a union rather than to join it'. Failure to recognise this explicitly in this work lends to arguments urgently relevant to the problems of the centres of Western civilisation an air of unreality and general inapplicability which deprives them of much of the force which, if more cautiously stated, they might have had."

The paper entitled "Liberalism and the International Problem", referred to above, is reprinted in my *Money, Trade and International Relations,* also published in 1971.

London School of Economics
June 1972   LIONEL ROBBINS

ECONOMIC PLANNING
AND
INTERNATIONAL ORDER

MACMILLAN AND CO., Limited
LONDON · BOMBAY · CALCUTTA · MADRAS
MELBOURNE

THE MACMILLAN COMPANY
NEW YORK · BOSTON · CHICAGO
DALLAS · ATLANTA · SAN FRANCISCO

THE MACMILLAN COMPANY
OF CANADA, LIMITED
TORONTO

ECONOMIC PLANNING
AND
INTERNATIONAL ORDER

BY

LIONEL ROBBINS

PROFESSOR OF ECONOMICS IN THE
UNIVERSITY OF LONDON

MACMILLAN AND CO., LIMITED
ST. MARTIN'S STREET, LONDON
1937

COPYRIGHT

PRINTED IN GREAT BRITAIN
BY R. & R. CLARK, LIMITED, EDINBURGH

TO
THE MEMORY
OF
EDWIN CANNAN

PREFACE

THESE chapters owe their origin to an invitation to lecture at the *Institut des Hautes Études Internationales* at Geneva in the summer of 1935. When the lectures had been delivered, it occurred to me that it might be worth while revising them for a wider public : and in the process of revision, while the outline has been preserved, something like a new book has emerged. I should like to take this opportunity of thanking Professor Rappard and the authorities of the *Institut* for their invitation and their hospitality. Parts of some of the chapters of the revised version have been published in a modified form in the *Quarterly Review of the Amsterdamsche Bank, Lloyds Bank Monthly Review, Ekonomista* and *The Banker*. I am indebted to the editors of these journals for the opportunity of thus securing discussion of certain of the views here presented.

The book is essentially an essay in what may be called Political Economy, as distinct from Economics in the stricter sense of the word. It depends upon the technical apparatus of analytical Economics ; but it applies this apparatus to the examination of schemes for the realization of aims whose formulation lies outside Economics; and it does not abstain from appeal to the probabilities of political practice when such an appeal has seemed relevant. At the same time it makes no attempt to discuss the *minutiae* of contemporary policy. I am not at all unwilling to do this. But the conditions which policy has to take account of change almost from day to day; and it seemed better to reserve their discussion for other places. The aim here has been to show the implications of different types of principle, not to prepare a programme of immediate action.

In attempting such a task I am under no illusions concerning the risks I am running. It is impossible, in an essay of this length in which every sentence necessarily involves a world of associations, to state explicitly all the assumptions on which it rests, or to discuss in detail all the reasons determining the choice of particular perspectives. I have tried very hard to be clear. But I do not hope altogether to have eliminated the possibility of misapprehension. I would plead, however, that before a verdict is passed upon any one section the argument should be read as a whole: the reasoning throughout is interconnected and full explanation of the earlier propositions is in some cases deliberately postponed in order to emphasize their connection with propositions which come later. In particular I would ask that readers who are disquieted by the critical tone of some of the earlier chapters should reserve judgment until they have read Chapters IX and XI, where I think I have something more positive to say. I would like at least to persuade my friends of the Left, who with me believe in reason and persuasion, that, although we may differ profoundly about means, we are at least at one in aiming at a common goal.

I have to thank various friends at the School of Economics and elsewhere who have helped me with information and criticism. I am indebted to Dr. Benham and Mr. Paish for advice on certain technical matters and to Mr. Paul Wilson for a most timely admonition. But in particular, my thanks are due to Professor Arnold Plant, who, in friendly disputation ever since we were students together, has taught me more about the various matters here discussed than I could easily acknowledge in detail. He is of course, in no way to be held responsible for any of my probably many blunders.

LIONEL ROBBINS

THE LONDON SCHOOL OF ECONOMICS
March 1937

CONTENTS

INTRODUCTION

CHAPTER I

THE OBJECT OF THE ESSAY   PAGE
1. The Meaning of Planning . . . 3
2. Object and Plan of the Essay . . . 7

PART I
INDEPENDENT NATIONAL PLANNING

CHAPTER II

THE NATURE OF NATIONAL PLANNING
1. Introduction 13
2. Protectionism as Planning . . . 14
3. The Transition to Socialism . . . 22
4. The Control of Investment . . . 29
5. The Monetary Policy of Economic Nationalism   33
6. The Restriction of Migration . . . 36

CHAPTER III

THE INTERNATIONAL SIGNIFICANCE OF NATIONAL PLANNING
1. Introduction 39
2. The International Significance of Tariffs . 41

		PAGE
3. Agrarian and Industrial Protectionism	.	47
4. The Quantitative Regulation of Trade	.	55
5. The Significance of Complete National Socialism	. . . . . .	60
6. The International Distribution of Capital under National Planning	. . .	68
7. The International Distribution of Labour under National Planning	. . .	71

CHAPTER IV

NATIONAL PLANNING AND INTERNATIONAL STABILITY

1. Introduction	. . . . .	74
2. Geographical Syndicalism and the Market	.	76
3. The Effects of Change in a World of Independent National Planning	. . .	80
4. The "Politicalization" of Trade	. .	90
5. The "Haves" and the "Have-nots" and Independent National Planning	. .	92

PART II

PARTIAL INTERNATIONAL PLANNING

CHAPTER V

TRADE AGREEMENTS AND REGIONAL GROUPING

1. Introduction	. . . . .	99
2. The Genesis of Bilateralism	. . .	100
3. The Economics of Bilateralism	. . .	102
4. The Effects of Bilateralism	. . .	108
5. International Sales Agreements	. .	111
6. Tariff Unions	. . . . .	116
7. The Colonial Question	. . . .	123

CONTENTS

CHAPTER VI

INTERNATIONAL PLANNING OF PARTICULAR LINES OF INDUSTRY

	PAGE
1. Introduction	129
2. The Genesis of International Restrictionism	130
3. The Economics of Restrictionism	134
4. The Politics of Restrictionism	141
5. The "*The* Industry" Fallacy	144
6. The Alleged Inevitability of the Concentration of the Control of Production	154

CHAPTER VII

INTERNATIONAL REGULATION OF WAGES AND HOURS OF LABOUR

1. Introduction	158
2. The Effects of International Equalization of Wage Rates	159
3. The Significance of International Wage Differences	166
4. Two Countries competing in a Third	174
5. The Effects of International Equalization of Hours	177
6. Real Incomes and Productivity	182

PART III

COMPLETE INTERNATIONAL PLANNING

CHAPTER VIII

INTERNATIONAL COMMUNISM

1. Introduction	187
2. The Literature of Planning	188

3. The Wants of the Consumer . . . 191
4. World Planning without World Markets . 194
5. Pseudo-Competition 205
6. International Communism and the Wage Problem 211
7. The Accumulation of Capital under International Communism 215
8. International Communism and Democracy . 219

CHAPTER IX

INTERNATIONAL LIBERALISM

1. Introduction 221
2. The Liberal Solution 221
3. Liberalism as Planning 223
4. The Anti-Liberal Reaction . . . 232
5. The Fundamental Requirement of International Liberalism 238
6. The Functions of "States" in a Liberal Federation 246
7. The Limitations of Liberalism . . . 258

CHAPTER X

INTERNATIONAL MONEY

1. Introduction 269
2. The Nature of the Transfer "Problem" . 270
3. The Theory of Monetary Nationalism . 280
4. Monetary Nationalism in Internationalist Clothing 290
5. International Money 299
6. The International Banking Problem . . 301

CONCLUSION

CHAPTER XI

NATIONALISM OR INTERNATIONALISM?

1. Introduction 309
2. Defence and Opulence 310
3. Protectionism 311
4. Migration and Nationalism . . . 316
5. The Aspirations of Keynes and Fichte . 319
6. Nationalism and Internationalism . . 324
7. Conclusion 326

SELECT BIBLIOGRAPHY 329

INTRODUCTION

CHAPTER I

THE OBJECT OF THE ESSAY

1. THE object of this essay is to discuss from an international point of view the economic significance of various types of planning.

But this statement, accurate enough as a label, does not really make sufficiently explicit the ground which it is intended to cover. " Planning" is the grand panacea of our age. But unfortunately its meaning is highly ambiguous. In popular discussion it stands for almost any policy which it is wished to present as desirable. Indeed there can be no doubt that it is this very ambiguity which lends it attractive force. Men do not cherish vague emotions about precise concepts. When the average citizen, be he Nazi or Communist or Summer School Liberal, warms to the statement that "What the world needs is planning", what he really feels is that the world needs that which is satisfactory. It is in fact almost certain that the more of a plan he is actually confronted with, the less general will be his emotion, the less likely his agreement with the other members of the crowd.

Now, strictly speaking, all economic life involves planning. Economic activity is activity involving the disposal of scarce goods; and the disposal of goods, in so far as it is in any way purposive, necessarily involves some kind of plan. The consumer spending his income, the producer arranging his output, the investor deciding how much to save and in what lines to invest it, are all planning. To plan is to act with purpose, to choose; and choice is the essence of economic activity.[1]

It is clear then that, no matter what the social system, we all plan in greater or less degree. But it is clear too that as soon as there is more than one individual planning, the different plans may not harmonize. If my plan and your plan involve using the same instruments, it may well be that, in the absence of co-ordination and authority, the one plan may be frustrated by the other. My plan may be realized by robbing you, yours by robbing me. The result of our separate planning may be disorder and chaos. To avoid this, to secure that social relations involve a greater realization of individual plans rather than their mutual frustration, a co-ordinating apparatus, a social order, a social plan is necessary. It is in this sense that the term plan figures in contemporary discussions of policy.

[1] I may perhaps be permitted to refer in this connection to my *Nature and Significance of Economic Science*, where these matters are treated in some detail.

But, this recognized, we are yet not very far advanced. For, on the necessity for some coordination, some limitation of the freedom of the individual, there is really very little disagreement. The liberal who believes that, given a suitable framework of law and order, spontaneous arrangements between private citizens will conduce to the public good, and the communist who believes that nothing but central control of all productive activities will achieve the same end, are at least in agreement on this, that there must be some coordinating authority with coercive power : their differences relate to the extent to which individual initiative may be left free. Even the anarchist who believes that no authority is necessary, that, provided there is no central apparatus of coercion, no arbitrary force will disturb the smooth conduct of mutually satisfactory private relations, even he believes in an order of a sort. It may be true that the logical conclusion of certain contemporary practices is the ultimate breaking off of all social relations. But this conclusion is seldom defended. Outspoken defence of the dissolution of the social bond, of the reversion to that state of nature where the life of man is solitary, poor, nasty, brutish and short, is a rare thing in human history.

It follows therefore that the question to plan or not to plan, so frequently posed nowadays, is essentially a red herring. It has not been seriously suggested that there should be no plan, no order in society. The issue is not between *a* plan and *no* plan, it is between different kinds of plan. To appropriate for one method of co-ordination a title which applies to all, may be excellent propaganda. But it is not conducive to a reasonable decision of the essential problem : which is the best method to choose. It may be that the liberal [1] plan of decentralizing much of the responsibility for the organization of production through the complex institutions of a system of private property is destined to be superseded by a plan which brings responsibility to the centre. But, if this is so, it will be the supersession of one plan by another, not the supersession of no plan by planning. We do not rise to the level of the momentous decisions with which we are confronted if we flatter ourselves with the belief that it is just a choice between deliberately willing order or chaos.

Nevertheless, we may freely recognize that the use of the term planning in recent discussion has had a more limited significance. The plans which have been urged on our attention have all had this characteristic in common, that they

[1] It should be clearly understood that the use of the term liberal throughout this essay has no necessary reference to the programme of any particular political party in Great Britain. It refers solely to a certain social philosophy. There can be little doubt that Mr. Lloyd George's agricultural plans would have been more antipathetic to the founders of European liberalism than many of the plans of the most radical socialist.

have involved much more limitation of individual planning than was contemplated under the plans favoured in the liberal epoch. Individual planning of consumption is not often called in question directly. But individual planning of production to meet the demands of consumers, this, in one way or another, is to be extensively curtailed, or indeed completely superseded. "Planning", in the modern jargon, involves governmental control of production in some form or other. It was the aim of the liberal plan to create a framework within which private plans might be harmonized. It is the aim of modern "planning" to supersede private plans by public—or at any rate to relegate them to a very subordinate position.

2. It is the object of this essay to discuss some of these plans and to contrast them with others which are yet conceivable. But it is proposed to discuss them from a special point of view, which must be made explicit here at the outset. Recent discussion of economic planning has tended to concentrate upon one of two aspects. Either it has been concerned with discussion of the effects of the planning of particular industries—the planning of British coal or the planning of agriculture, for instance. Or it has discussed the general question of the practicability of a society completely planned from the centre—the problem of the economics of a closed socialist (or com-

munist) community. Both these enquiries are important. But, even together, they suffer from a certain lack of actuality. Discussion of plans for particular industries is obviously incomplete. If pushed to its logical conclusion it must involve discussion of general planning : as we shall see later on, the " planning " of particular industries almost inevitably tends to spread. On the other hand, the problems which arise when it actually does spread are hardly exhausted by abstract discussion of the problems of pure collectivism. For, in the world we live in, planning is done by states ; and the authority of each different state is not co-extensive with the total sphere of world economic activity. National planning takes place in an international *milieu*. We leave out of the picture some of its most important problems if we omit its international implications and discuss merely what happens when " *the* " state does this or " *the* " government does that. Moreover, even if we assume, as it is useful for certain purposes to assume, that the present anarchy of interstate relations is removed and one state only exists, we yet do not do justice to the nature of the problem unless we keep continually in mind a state of the extent and complexity of the world as it actually is, with its present distribution and variety of resources, its vast population and the varying density of this population in different places. The problem of collectivism is in this sense a practical one. It is clear that a small community, a patriarchal family or a small tribe, can be run on collectivist lines with no breakdown of the mechanism of economic calculation. The problem with which the twentieth century is confronted is whether a similar solution is possible for a community of world dimensions.

For all these reasons it seems worth while examining the significance of different kinds of planning from a specifically international point of view—a point of view at once more general than discussion of the particular effects of isolated acts of national planning and less abstract than discussion of the economics of the closed socialist community. It is this which is the intention of this essay. The argument will fall into three main parts. In the first will be discussed the tendencies and the significance of independent national planning. In the second will be discussed various proposals for international controls of particular sections of the economic field, international agreements regarding trade, international regulations of particular lines of production, international regulation of conditions of labour. Finally, in the third, an attempt will be made to discuss the problems of complete international planning on both socialist and liberal lines. Throughout these sections the standpoint adopted is international. The various plans examined are judged according to their effects on the welfare of humanity as a whole. It is assumed that the citizens of different states may be regarded as members of one general world community. The criterion of rational planning is assumed to be conformity to the requirements of an international order. In a concluding chapter, an attempt is made to decide in what sense there may be conflict between these requirements and the interests of the different national groups. Naturally nowhere will the treatment pretend to exhaustiveness. The aim throughout is to see the main problems in their proper proportions, not to examine them in all their detail.

PART I

INDEPENDENT NATIONAL PLANNING

CHAPTER II

THE NATURE OF NATIONAL PLANNING

1. OUR first task, according to the programme just outlined, is to examine the international significance of independent national planning—using planning in this context to mean collective control or supersession of private activities of production and exchange.

In a sense, therefore, our first task is a survey of the contemporary world position. Current discussion often suggests that the adoption of national planning in the sense just indicated is still an open question. But this is not so. Our age is an age of independent national planning. The degree of completeness of different systems varies greatly, from the totalitarian planning of Soviet Russia on the one hand, to the exchange controls and marketing boards of the outlying raw material producing areas on the other. The object, too, varies greatly. In some cases the plans are designed quite deliberately to supplant the institutions of the free market. In others they are the more or less haphazard resultant of desperate attempts to meet the exigencies of what is believed to be a transitory emergency. The fact remains, however, that at the present day control by the different national authorities of the main processes of economic activity is rapidly becoming the rule rather than the exception. This process has been greatly accelerated in the recent depression. In many ways the most conspicuous feature of the upswing which has taken place since the low point of 1931–32 has been the extent to which recovery in different parts of the world has been national rather than international—the product of local policy rather than of general revival. At the present time there is not one trade cycle but many, each no doubt in the last resort still influenced by external conditions, but, in origin and degree of development, each different from the others. The real question is, not whether national planning should be adopted, but rather what happens now that it is a dominant feature of the international situation.

2. The most obvious instrument of national planning in the sphere of international business is the tariff. It has the longest history and the most general usage. Whether in fact the tariff systems of the mercantilist era had the coherence of plans may be debated. But there is no question that they were defended as such by contemporary writers : and it is significant that the

nineteenth-century historians, such as Schmoller or Cunningham, who were the intellectual leaders of the attack on international liberalism, based their apology for the revival of mercantilist practices on the ground that the essence of mercantilism was national planning. At the present time such practices are general. Since the abandonment of free trade by Great Britain, there is no example of an important Power which does not have recourse to tariffs as a means of regulating its relations with the outside world. We all have " scientific " tariffs now.

The objects of such regulations are, however, various. In the heyday of mercantilism, chief emphasis was laid upon the accumulation of treasure. If it could be so arranged that year by year the nation contracted less obligations to pay money abroad than were contracted with it, then, it was thought, there would result an inflow of the precious metals, with highly beneficial effects all round. " The ordinary means . . . to encrease our wealth and treasure is by *Forraign Trade* wherein wee must ever observe this rule, to sell more to strangers yearly than wee consume of theirs in value," said Thomas Mun, whose book, we are told, was the Bible of Mercantilism. Much scorn has been poured on this policy by nineteenth-century writers, on the ground that it mistook money for wealth, a store of the precious metals for general well-being. But this is altogether too simple. Whether we like this policy or not, we must give its educated apologists credit for rather more intelligence than this. And indeed it seems clear that, in the last analysis, their concern with the precious metals and the balance of trade was not at all dissimilar from that of many recent writers on these subjects. They were anxious to secure the benefits of local inflation. If the balance of payments were favourable, if " wee sold more to strangers than wee consumed of theirs in value ", there would be an inflow of the precious metals, the circulation would increase, trade would become brisk and the nation would be prosperous. Our terminology is more sophisticated nowadays. But there is really no essential difference here from the arguments with which English economists broke down the resistance to tariffs in 1931—save that the mercantilists do not appear to have urged that turning the balance of trade in our favour would bring great benefits to *other* nations.

In the years between the publication of *The Wealth of Nations* and the *Proposals for a Revenue Tariff*, however, these arguments were not held in great esteem by competent authorities. The contradictions implicit in the spectacle of a world in which the government of each nation attempted by means of tariffs to turn the balance of trade in its favour, had more weight with the economists of those times than considerations of the momen-

CH. II NATURE OF NATIONAL PLANNING

tary advantages which might be snatched from such a policy. It was realized that the inflationary stimulus of the imposition of a tariff depended essentially upon the refusal of other nations to pursue a like course. It was realized too that such a stimulus was soon spent and that, in order that it might continue, a continuous rise in the tariff was essential. Hence the defence of tariffs as a means of securing a favourable balance of trade was left to the lesser lights of political journalism; and those apologists for tariffs who wished to be taken seriously by educated people had recourse to other arguments.

The first and the most considerable of all these arguments was the celebrated "infant industry argument" which sprang from the work of Hamilton and List. It was held by these writers that while complete freedom of trade was the appropriate commercial policy for " developed " nations, it was desirable at a certain stage that the growth of manufacturing industry should be promoted by protective duties. Once the infant was mature the duty should be discarded. But during the process of growth, it was said, protection was in the general interest. Throughout the nineteenth century this argument was made the pretext for a vast structure of policy. In the United States, in Germany, in those of the British Colonies which achieved tariff autonomy, the alleged necessity for building up national industry was made the pretext for high protective duties—duties, it should be said, which, contrary to the Listian prescription, it was found necessary to maintain long after the infants had grown to gigantic proportions. Since the war, with the carving out of new nations by the treaties, new areas have been found to be deficient in manufacturing industries. In the secession states of Central Europe and in the Irish Free State, a virtual exclusion of competing foreign products has been necessary to bring the somewhat recalcitrant local infants to birth. No doubt were the principality of Wales or the duchy of Cornwall to obtain the much-prized powers of self-determination, similar arguments would be invoked in support of similar policies.

The protection of domestic manufacture, however, leaves large sections of the community unprivileged. As the nineteenth century wore on, as the development of mechanical transport brought food products from areas where land was very cheap to areas where it was still very dear, it began to be felt, especially by the landlords of the latter areas, that a new field for national planning lay open. In the nineties, particularly in France and Germany, there arose a school of thought, of which Adolf Wagner was the outstanding representative, which held that it was in the interests of the state that industrialization should not be allowed to go " too far ". List held that it was uneconomic to have " too little " manufacture, Wagner that it was uneconomic to have " too much ". Being unwilling to urge the invalidity of the arguments for industrial protection, he therefore urged the erection of protective duties on agricultural imports, on the ground that by such a policy a " due balance " would be secured between the various branches of the national economy. This argument has enjoyed great popularity. The idea of a balance between industry and agriculture, although, as we shall see, lacking much in precision, has afforded a basis on which the most exacting claims of the agricultural and industrial interests appear to be reconcilable without concession to the " extremism " of free trade. If in doubt, raise *all* tariffs. In the years since the war, when the application of scientific technique to various branches of agriculture has greatly diminished the labour necessary to produce a given output, the alleged necessity of maintaining a certain proportionate distribution of effort between agriculture and industry has led to the erection of obstacles to the diminution of agricultural prices whose dimensions are truly remarkable. To maintain the "due balance" between the interests of agriculture and industry in Germany, the unfortunate consumers are compelled to pay for the elementary necessities of life prices, in some cases fifty, in some cases a hundred and in some cases two or even three hundred per cent higher than the prices outside the boundary. The detached observer—if such still exists in that miserable country—may easily conceive the benefits of such a balance to the pockets of the landlords and the peasantry. But he may well wonder whether, to the unfortunate industrial worker, the spectacle of so many extra hectares of land under cultivation is a substantial compensation for the other goods and services which he might have procured had the price of food been lower.

The argument for tariffs, as instruments for promoting "due balance" within the national economy, has long transcended the original dreams of agricultural enthusiasts. The fostering of the manufacture of crude steel, the production of dolls' eyes, the consumption of home-grown rhubarb, have all been found to be capable of defence by the same elastic argument. There is one group of industries, however, to which tariffs, as such, are obviously not applicable, the industries catering predominantly for export. A protective tariff can do nothing to sustain exports which are unable to compete on foreign markets. It can do nothing to guard against competition abroad.

In such circumstances, however, the type of planning we are considering is not helpless. It cannot charge duties on imports into *foreign* markets. But it can subsidize the domestic industry which competes with these imports. The bounty on export is the complement of the duty on import.

Within limits such a policy is often adopted. The interventionist states, unwilling to see their shipowners too much embarrassed by their own and other people's tariffs, have not infrequently subsidized shipping. Special railway rates have been offered to exporters using state railways; and in many other ways concealed subsidies have been paid to exporters. But clearly the practical limit to this sort of thing is much lower than the limit to protective duties. For the subsidy costs money; and the extent to which the average voter is willing to see the taxes he pays devoted to subsidizing particular industries is very much less than the extent to which he is willing to forgo the advantages of cheap purchases from abroad. Perhaps this is short-sighted. My real income is depleted as much if I pay ten pounds a year more for bacon because I am forced to buy bacon from home producers, as if I hand over an extra ten pounds a year to the income-tax authorities to be given to the owners of tramp steamers. But the fact is that I am much more likely to squeal at the higher tax than at the higher price, and this sets a limit to policy. The export subsidy only plays a large rôle when it can be indirectly granted by differential exchange depreciation. This instrument is of very recent invention. At the present time it is chiefly used in Germany. It must await the next depression before it is more widely adopted.

3. It follows from all this that we must not underestimate the extent to which tariffs and subsidies may be conceived as instruments of national planning. To English radicals, brought up in the tradition of regarding all tariffs as conspiracies against the public weal, such a view must seem highly paradoxical. But it is not so. It is quite true that the various tariff systems have frequently, indeed usually, been perverted by sinister interest. But we simplify matters unduly if we suppose that all the plans which have been thus perverted, have had necessarily a sinister origin. However much we may disagree with their views, we do not get things in proper perspective if we are not willing to assume that the leading apologists for tariffs have been honest men, sincerely anxious for the public good. Nor is the accusation of class bias any more admissible. It is true that, in Great Britain, support of tariffs has usually come from the Right. But elsewhere, even in English-speaking countries, the bias has often been reversed. In Australia, to take a conspicuous example, the protection of manufacturing industry has been nowhere supported more strongly than by Labour. In India the leading progressives are for the most part Listian protectionists. We shall not get correct views on this very difficult subject if we are not willing to shake off ancient prejudice sufficiently to enable us to see protectionism (including sub-

sidies) as a leading species of the genus national plan.

It must be admitted, however, that it is a very mild form of planning. The tariff imposes certain obstacles to trade. But within this framework of obstacles the disposition of capital and labour is still uncontrolled from the centre. The organization of production is still free. Provided that the duty is paid, even the goods which are taxed may come in. It is as though the national area imposing the tariff had moved further away from other areas : or that the cost of moving goods between areas had been enhanced by greater inefficiency of transport in respect of the commodities protected. Naturally this means a different distribution of productive resources. It is just in this that the planning consists. It is more profitable to produce the commodities protected or subsidized, less profitable to put money into other forms of production. But, given the new conditions, production is still guided by the market. Private enterprise is not superseded. The sphere within which it plans is limited still further than under free trade. Certain opportunities of profit, certain economies in the use of the factors of production, are ruled out. But a considerable degree of private planning still persists.

It follows, therefore, that planning by tariffs is not likely to be acceptable to the advocates of complete planning from the centre. Within the limits prescribed by the tariff system, it leaves the organization of production under private direction; and it is the main contention of the advocates of central planning that "individualistic" organization of production is inefficient. Against this belief the protectionist must necessarily argue at a disadvantage. He has admitted that private enterprise by itself will not guide productive resources into what he regards as the "best" channels. How then can he argue that, within the limits prescribed by the tariff, its operations will necessarily be efficient? To the dogmatic believer in the essential inefficiency of any production which is not planned from the centre, the kind of planning involved by the tariff will seem a very poor half-way house.

Moreover, even from the point of view of the protectionist, such measures are not always very effective instruments. The object of the tariff or the subsidy is to prevent the proportion of factors of production devoted to certain kinds of industry falling below a certain figure by reason of the competition of cheap imports—to prevent the "extinction of agriculture", "the annihilation of the iron and steel trades", etc. etc. etc. In quiet times of slow change it may be reasonably effective for this purpose. But if technique is changing rapidly, or if there occur large dislocations on account of other people's tariffs, it may well happen that it breaks down. To prevent the industry which it is desired to protect from being " ruined by a flood of cheap imports ", a tariff may be completely ineffective. To stop the cheap imports in such circumstances, not tariffs but prohibitions are necessary. It is in this way that import quotas have sometimes been born. This is indeed the official apology for the quotas on agricultural imports now in vogue in continental Europe.[1] Similarly with subsidies to export. If markets are severely disorganized, the magnitude of subsidy necessary becomes an intolerable burden.

For all these reasons, in the modern world there is a tendency to go beyond tariffs and subsidies in the planning of production. Particular branches of industry are nationalized just because it is thought they should be planned. The volume of different types of imports is subject to quantitative control on the ground that tariffs would be inadequate. The business of export is centralized in the hope of favourably affecting the value of sales.

Moreover each tendency reinforces the other. It is clearly conceivable that there should exist control schemes without import quotas or import quotas without control of domestic production. But such arrangements are not likely to happen. There is a strong probability that, whichever way

[1] For a good account of the genesis of the French import quota system see Haight, *French Import Quotas.*

the start is made, and whatever motive is operative, one type of control will involve the others. Thus it is possible to conceive nationalized industry which is left free to face foreign competition. But it is not likely that we shall see such an experiment. Suppose that it were decided to nationalize the Lancashire cotton industry. It is conceivable that it might be decided to continue to permit free (or lightly taxed) imports of cotton goods from abroad. But it is much more probable that the controlling authority would be given the monopoly of the domestic market. It would surely be thought unwise that so bold an experiment in socialism should be jeopardized by the " wanton " import of cheap goods from Japan.

In exactly the same way, if the thing starts by the quantitative control of imports, it is highly probable that it will lead to control of domestic industry. It will lead to control of the mechanism of import. The allotment of licences to hitherto competing importers is administratively so difficult and involves so many anomalies that there is a strong incentive to go the whole hog and set up some sort of collective buying apparatus—an import board—to deal with matters as a whole. It will lead, too, to control of the production of the commodity protected. If the aim is to restore prosperity to a particular branch of industry, it would be "fatal" to allow the market to be depressed by the entry of new capital to the industry. We see this tendency operative in the British experiments in agricultural planning. In the Hop Scheme, which is logically the most advanced and coherent, it has been found necessary to supplement arrangements for collective marketing and (informal) control of imports by licensing of production. Indeed the ideas of planning domestic production and quantitative control of import and export are necessarily intimately connected. They are complementary halves of a common policy of planning. The British Ministry of Agriculture has been strongly criticized for the view expressed in the Report on the Reorganization of Pig Marketing that the merits of quotas as instruments of long-term planning have as yet been inadequately appreciated: and if we have regard to the havoc which has been worked in recent times by the growth of such regulations, such criticism may seem to be justified. But from the point of view of men who were determined to bring about the socialization of British agriculture, the proposition was completely consistent. State control of domestic industry and quantitative control of import and export are almost inseparably connected.

Now this type of planning, even more than planning by tariffs and subsidies, has a tendency to spread. We all know that if one industry is given the protection of a tariff, many others will clamour for like favours. It is possible, however, that a strong government may resist this pressure. The tariff is part of a plan, they may urge. To erect others would tend to nullify its effects. Austerities of this sort are certainly rare in history. But they are not completely impracticable.

But with the more full-blooded type of planning we are now discussing, things are different. The quantitative control of foreign trade or domestic production seems to involve a sort of principle of multiplication. To control effectively in one line it is necessary to extend control in others. During the war it was found that if the state assumed control in one small section of industry, it was rapidly compelled, in order to give effect to its policy, to control all branches of industry remotely connected with it. In exactly the same way, in peace-time, if the government assumes control of one branch of agriculture and agricultural imports, it is not long before the repercussions of this policy bring into being a situation in which it is necessary to control other branches. If the import of milk products is restricted, then internal production of milk for manufacturing purposes increases. If this is not to break the market it is necessary to control production—that is to say, to limit the amount of capital and labour that may be devoted to this branch of farming. But if this is done, then the capital and labour which is outside the charmed circle will cry also for loaves and fishes. And this pressure is much more difficult to resist than more pressure for a tariff. For in the case of the tariff it can be said: " For reasons of state we have encouraged this branch of industry. We see no reasons to encourage yours. Your misfortunes are due to general causes which we think it would be unwise to attempt to control." But in the case of the quota-plus-domestic-licence system, this kind of argument will not do. For the misfortunes of the complainants are due to domestic policy. The prohibition of investments in the planned area means that those excluded have to be content with a lower return outside. The Minister may turn the deputation from the door. But it will be very hard for him to do so. Planning of this sort is a quicksand. You may intend to step ever so lightly. But you are almost certain to be drawn in completely. The thorough carrying-out of the planning of particular industries sooner or later involves the planning of most of the others.

4. At the present day this process has gone far. The extension of government control both of domestic production and of foreign trade proceeds apace. In the sphere of foreign trade it proceeds much more by the limitation of imports than by the control of exports. The one is so much more simple than the other. Moreover it is what domestic producers demand. But since the im-

ports of one area are the exports of another, it is possible greatly to exaggerate the freedom of the export trade from some form of government control. There are still large areas of economic activity where state planning of the kind we are discussing is not operative directly. But they are very much less than they were five years ago; and their size is still diminishing.

But the tendency to national planning does not stop short at the control of established lines of industry. The creation of new industry is also to be regulated. One of the main aims of national planning, in the contemporary sense of the word, is the regulation of long-term investment, especially of foreign investment.

Now some control of individual investment is not a new thing. In Great Britain, up to the outbreak of the Great War, it was rare. But in continental Europe, foreign investment, at least, was often subjected to a considerable degree of regulation. International financial operations were made subservient to the obscure devices of balance-of-power diplomacy.[1] The savings of the French peasants cemented the Franco-Russian alliance. The making of treaties and the granting of loans were often complementary operations.

But the kind of control now contemplated

---

[1] Marxian readers should note the sequence. So far as investment in Europe was concerned, finance followed politics, not politics finance. See Feis, *Europe the World's Banker*, passim.

CH. II NATURE OF NATIONAL PLANNING 31

is quite different. The pre-war control had a limited political objective. The post-war control has wide-sweeping economic aims. It seeks to control not merely isolated investments but the whole mechanism of long-term lending. Nor can it be conceived to stop at that. Sooner or later it involves nothing less than the complete nationalization of the whole mechanism of lending and borrowing. Not merely the long-term, but even the short-term market, must also eventually be planned.

We can see this very clearly if we examine the tendencies operative. The roots of the movements are twofold. On the one hand, it springs from the general distrust of the workings of the free market : free capital, it is thought, should go where the national authorities decide, not where expectations of profitability lead it. On the other hand, it is the outcome of the increasing participation by states in particular lines of industry. If a state has invested resources in a particular industry it is most improbable that it will allow competition from within its own borders. Investment in that line is therefore prohibited, save by permit. If the British Government has guaranteed investment in a Cunarder, it prohibits the acquisition of Red Star liners for a competitive enterprise. If this sort of thing becomes general, the field of free investment becomes limited. The rate of return on new investment tends to fall. A demand arises that the state itself shall provide new openings for capital. Thus, both negatively and positively, the part played by the state in the control of long-term investment tends to increase.

But this is not all. The control of long-term investment cannot be made effective so long as only new issues are controlled. The regulation must be much more far-reaching. Let us suppose that a national investment board is set up with the object of controlling new issues. For reasons into which we need not enquire, it decides to prohibit the flotation of a certain foreign loan. What happens ? In the absence of further control, the issue is likely to be made in another centre. Then when the commissions have been made by foreign houses, it will be sold to the citizens of the state where new investment is controlled, *via* the mechanism of the stock markets. Unless the control is to be ineffective, it must be extended. The stock exchange list, that is to say the market in old securities, must also be controlled.

But this also will not be effective unless the control goes further still. If I cannot buy the security I want, either on the market for new issues or on the stock exchange at home, I transfer my money abroad and buy it on a foreign stock exchange. It follows, therefore, that foreign transfer too must be controlled. It must be made impossible for me to acquire a balance abroad if I propose to use it for ends which defeat the purpose of the National Investment Authority. If therefore it is not to be merely nominal, the control of new investment leads, not merely to the control of the purchase of old securities, but also to control of the foreign exchanges. The British Government, which has recently been dabbling in the control of investment, not so much with any deliberately industrial plan in mind as with a view to manipulating the market for its own conversion operations, has been lucky. The risks of the position elsewhere have imposed so great a check on foreign investment of any kind that only the mildest of regulations has been necessary to secure its limited objective. But let prosperity return elsewhere, say by means of a thoroughgoing boom on Wall Street, and it will need more than polite restraints on new issues to prevent money rates from hardening.

5. This tendency to the planning of the capital market is very powerfully reinforced by other tendencies in the sphere of monetary policy.

The provision of a satisfactory money is a matter which has usually involved some degree of planning from the centre. Arrangements are of course conceivable whereby, as in China under the silver standard, the commodity used as money is supplied by private enterprise and tested by the scrutiny of users. But the use of money by weight rather than by tale is an obvious inconvenience ; and even in a system of purely metallic coinage it has usually been thought desirable that the state should play some part by regulating the nature and the quality of the unit. As the credit system developed, regulation by the national authority has been thought to be more and more essential.

But, speaking broadly, it may be said that, up to the war, the trend of development was more and more in the direction of an international money. We must except from this statement certain developments in the sphere of banking policy which we shall have occasion to discuss later.[1] But in the main the trend was international. One by one the different states brought their currency arrangements into the framework of the international gold standard. They deliberately planned an international money.

Since the war all this has changed. Partly as a result of the financial difficulties of the ex-belligerents, partly as a result of a desire for autonomy as regards the price level, partly in response to a demand for public expenditure to create employment, many of the chief Powers have ceased even the pretence of adjusting their policies to the exigencies of the international plan. They have expanded when the balance of payments was against them. They have refrained from contracting when prices and costs within their area

[1] See Chapter X, para. 6, below.

CH. II NATURE OF NATIONAL PLANNING

were out of international equilibrium. They have resorted to exchange manipulation to produce revival from depression.

It is obvious that all this is quite incompatible with the maintenance of an international money —other than bar gold privately hoarded. The attempt to work the gold standard on these nationalistic lines broke down quite definitely in 1931. Since then, although there are still some who pretend that it is possible to have both the benefits of an international and a national money at once, the most enlightened advocates of national monetary autonomy perceive that it involves inevitably the abandonment of the regime of fixed exchanges.

It involves much more than this. It involves central control of the foreign exchange market. The movements of a completely free exchange are very disconcerting. They provide, even for day-to-day business, a medium of exchange which is highly unstable. It follows therefore that, even if actual control of individual transactions is not immediately resorted to, attempts will be made to introduce a limited stability by extensive buying and selling by exchange equalization funds and the like. It is highly improbable that the evening out, even of day-to-day fluctuations, will be left to a free market.

But such devices are only effective within limits. An exchange equalization fund can only produce stability within the limits of its own resources. If the tide sets strongly in one direction there comes a point at which it must give up the fight. It is no accident that in those areas where there has been real danger of a flight of capital, exchange dealing by the central authority has been found quite inadequate to produce the stability desired. Here again we should be careful of regarding recent British experience as typical. The extraordinary prudence of the Bank of England, together with the extraordinary risks of capital investment outside Great Britain, have brought it about that the operations of the Exchange Equalization Fund have been reasonably effective. Given different conditions elsewhere and a central bank of less conservative habits, it is almost certain they would have broken down. A government, bent on an expansionist policy regardless of external conditions, but unwilling to see an indefinite depreciation of the external value of its money, would be compelled to resort to thoroughgoing control of the exchanges. Not the loose and informal discipline of the London money market but the highly efficient controls of Dr. Schacht are the model for the planned state of the future.

6. There is a further feature of national planning which has hitherto almost completely escaped notice, although, if we take the secular view,

CH. II NATURE OF NATIONAL PLANNING 37

it is probably the most important. It involves the complete control of migration.[1] National planning involves not merely the suspension of *laissez faire* as regards movements of trade and investment. It involves also the suspension of *laissez passer* as regards the movements of men.

The reason for this is obvious. Even before the war, with certain developments of the social services, it was becoming clear that, if a state or a local government authority provided for the inhabitants of the area concerned a substantially higher level of uncharged benefits than were provided elsewhere, steps would have to be taken to prevent immigration. It would be resented if the taxable capacity of Great Britain were to be exhausted for the benefit of immigrants from Central Europe.

What was true of pre-war social reform naturally applies *a fortiori* to post-war planning. Only the *citizen* of a planned economy is entitled to work or maintenance. If national planning raises the standard of life, it is important that the increase should not be absorbed by immigration. If it lowers it, then immigration would only make

[1] It did not escape the notice of Edwin Cannan, who devoted one of the most original of his pre-war essays to the subject: "The Incompatibility of Socialism and Nationalism", *The Economic Outlook*, pp. 281-297. Cannan was temperamentally an optimist and hoped for the growth of international sentiment to remove the obstacles to which he drew attention. But it would not be too much to say that the salient features of the post-war Nazification of Europe are outlined in this short essay.

things worse. Even if market principles of remuneration still obtain, the argument for restriction is all-powerful. In the planned economy the labour market is protected.

For such reasons the victims of continental terrorism, unless possessed of influence, of capital, or of special technical qualifications not possessed by local labour, must be shipped back to "the country of origin".

CHAPTER III

THE INTERNATIONAL SIGNIFICANCE OF NATIONAL PLANNING

1. It is not difficult to see that the immediate effect on the world at large of the introduction of such measures as we have been discussing may be very gravely disturbing. The history of the last few years provides us with abundant examples. The multiplication of tariffs and quotas, the control of capital movements, the manipulation of the foreign exchanges, have had highly deflationary consequences. Indeed, it is no exaggeration to attribute both the severity of the depression and the somewhat precarious nature of the recovery which has followed to the existence of influences of this sort.[1] The dislocation in the established channels of trade which has been brought about by the recovery policies of the various states has been such that it would have been a miracle if it had been otherwise.

---

[1] In a recent work on post-war economic history, *The Great Depression*, I have attempted to demonstrate this in some detail. See especially chaps. iv and vi.

It would be possible to dwell at some length on all this. But at this stage it is not desirable to do so. For it is the purpose of our enquiry to investigate principles rather than particular cases. And although there are profound reasons for believing that the present troubles of the world are symptomatic of a state of affairs that may become permanent if present tendencies persist, yet it is desirable to examine these tendencies unimpeded by consideration of what may be merely transitional difficulties. Let us therefore attempt to examine the consequences of such policies without at first enquiring too closely whether they can even be introduced on a thorough-going scale without leading to grave difficulty. We may conduct our enquiry most appropriately under the groupings developed in the last chapter. We may examine the international consequences of the national planning of the movement of goods, of capital and of men. In this chapter we shall be concerned with the effects of such planning on the general distribution of resources — the "set-up", as it were, of the world apparatus of production. We shall be asking to what extent the operation of national controls of this kind is likely to lead to what, from the international point of view, is to be regarded as a rational disposition of productive power. How far does it lead to the application of effort at the points of maximum return ? Having done this, we shall

CH. III SIGNIFICANCE OF NATIONAL PLANNING 41

then be free, in the next chapter, to examine some of the more dynamic tendencies of such a system.

2. Let us turn first to the planning of trade; and let us first examine the international significance of tariffs. We can then pass by an easy transition to more rigorous forms of planning.[1]

If we review things in the large, it should be fairly clear that the effect of national protection is a diminution of international trade. We may admit the possibility that, owing to the imposition of tariffs on one class of commodity, markets elsewhere for other commodities may become so congested that new international outlets are sought. We may admit, too, that it is conceivable that the threat of the imposition of tariffs by one nation may lead to the lowering of tariffs by others— although, at this time of day, the suggestion that this sort of thing usually happens is not really very plausible. But speaking broadly there can be no doubt that tariffs, like obstacles to navigation, tend to diminish trade.

[1] It will be observed that the argument of the following sections surveys ground already covered very often by the classical discussion of free trade and protection. But it surveys it from a different point of view. The classical argument concentrates on the advantage or disadvantage of protective duties to the inhabitants of particular areas. There will be something to be said about this in the last chapter of the essay. But in this chapter the argument is directed to establishing the *international* significance of such restrictions. Unless this is borne in mind, certain differences between the present and the classical discussion are likely to be misunderstood.

Now it is just as well that we should have clear ideas of the concrete significance for the world of today of a substantial diminution of international commerce. It means the decline of shipping. When Mr. Keynes, the other day, urged that " goods should be homespun wherever it is reasonably and conveniently possible "[1], he was urging that the ports of the world should be allowed to decay and that ships and international railways should be devoted chiefly to carrying passengers. It means, therefore, the decline as centres of international trade of such cities as London, Liverpool, Amsterdam, Hamburg, Shanghai, Alexandria. The lively bustle of the great *entrepôts* must cease " wherever it is reasonably or conveniently possible ". It means, too, the decline of all those industries which have specialized in producing for export, the agriculture of the New World, the manufactures of the Old. The Lancashire cotton industry must henceforward look chiefly to home markets. British engineering must no longer seek a market in foreign parts. For a very long time to come, national planning in this sense means, not merely the protection of home industry, it must also mean the creation of depressed areas. The limitation of imports necessarily means the limitation of exports. It may not always be true, as the popular free-trade argument has sometimes suggested, that the limitation of imports into a

[1] " National Self-Sufficiency ", *Yale Review*, vol. xxii. p. 755.

CH. III SIGNIFICANCE OF NATIONAL PLANNING 43

particular area necessarily means an exactly commensurate limitation of exports from that area. But it certainly does mean a commensurate limitation of exports from *other* areas. For the imports of one area are the exports of other areas and if all areas limit imports, they limit exports also. The " depressed areas " are largely a by-product of economic nationalism.

But this consideration is not decisive unless international trade is to be regarded as an end in itself. And clearly it is not this: it is merely a means to an end, the satisfaction of demand. The function of international trade is not to maintain the export trades regardless of the demand for their products: it is to satisfy demand more adequately. If it could be shown that the contraction of international trade was conducive to more effective satisfaction of demand, more effective use of the productive resources of mankind, then, despite the agonies of the transition, it might be regarded as a change to be welcomed.

But this is not so. A contraction of international trade which is due, not to spontaneous changes in the direction of demand, but to the imposition of obstacles, must mean that the factors of production are used less efficiently, that demand in general is satisfied less adequately, than otherwise would be the case. For the restriction of trade means the restriction of the international division of labour. And the restriction of the international division of labour means that the cost of production is greater, the variety of products is less, than circumstances other than the obstacles necessitate. It means that the wrong goods are produced in the wrong places and that demand which could have been met goes unsatisfied. There may be those who gain from such a restriction as there are those who gain from earthquakes and shipwrecks. But their gain is an increased share of a volume of production which is less than might otherwise have been the case. And if earthquakes and shipwrecks become general, the probability of eventual individual gain becomes small. Who can seriously believe that the world at large is richer as a result of the various national restrictions which have led to the present contraction of international trade?

It is important to be clear on this point. It is sometimes thought that the advantages of international trade and the division of labour which it makes possible, are confined to the exchange of those products which it is impossible to produce "at home". The different nations should produce all that they can within their own borders, it is said. But beyond that, there is an advantage in procuring by way of exchange, commodities which, for geological or climatic reasons, it is *impossible* to produce at home. It is thought to be highly enlightened to urge the national authorities that protection can go "too far".

CH. III SIGNIFICANCE OF NATIONAL PLANNING 45

The import of pepper is advantageous ; only the import of pigs is a mistake.

But this is a misapprehension. The advantages of division of labour do not consist merely in permitting us to obtain by way of exchange *only* those things which we cannot produce for ourselves. They consist rather in permitting us to obtain by way of exchange *everything* save those commodities which we are best at producing. The advantages of international division of labour are essentially that it permits the inhabitants of each area to concentrate the application of their resources on those lines of production in which they are most efficient, getting what else they want for their own consumption by way of exchange with abroad. If each produces what he can best contribute to the common pool, the common pool is a maximum relative to the opportunities available. Costs are lower, prices are less, than otherwise would be the case.[1]

This rule is completely general. It applies quite clearly to the case where the inhabitants of different areas have differences of absolute efficiency at different kinds of production. It is obviously sensible for the inhabitants of Sheffield to concentrate on the production of high-grade steel and

[1] It is of course true that in certain circumstances (see Chapter XI) the imposition of a tariff may turn the terms of trade in favour of a particular area. But if it does so, the terms of trade are *ipso facto* turned against the rest of the world. From the international point of view the case falls into the categories of the general theory of monopoly.

to abstain from attempting to force bananas in glass-houses, and for the inhabitants of tropical areas to concentrate on the production of bananas and to leave high-grade steel products to centres more favourably situated. But our rule applies no less to the case where the advantages of absolute efficiency are all on one side. It might well be the case that the fertility of certain sites in the City of London was greater than the fertility of lands in East Anglia. But nevertheless it would not be sensible to use them for growing wheat. It is better that they should be used for the purposes for which their efficiency is greatest, leaving the wheat to be grown elsewhere. To employ resources in any but their most valuable use involves waste; that is to say, it involves satisfying less demand in price terms than would otherwise be possible.

Now it is just this diversion of resources from their most productive uses which is the effect of protective tariffs. If, under competitive conditions and reasonably full employment, the cost of producing an article in a certain area is greater than the price it fetches in the world market, it follows that there are other lines of production in that area which offer more valuable results. The fact that costs are above prices means that the prices of other products which can be produced in that area permit a higher remuneration of the factors of production than the prices of this product would warrant. If the price of wheat is such as to make growing wheat on urban sites an unremunerative enterprise, that is because the other uses to which the site can be put command a higher value in the market. If wages are too high for certain lines of domestic agriculture to be profitable, that means, under competitive conditions, that the labour in question can produce a higher value elsewhere. If a protective duty is imposed which so raises the prices of imports [1] competing with a certain line of business that business in that line becomes profitable, it follows that the factors of production there are devoted to producing something which, in the absence of the duty, would be less valuable, in preference to something which would be more valuable. It is this which is meant when it is said that protection involves discrimination against export. It brings it about that relatively more resources are employed producing directly for home consumption, relatively less producing for home consumption *indirectly*, by producing for export things to exchange for commodities produced abroad. It is thus that the international division of labour is diminished.

3. We can see this very vividly if we consider the results of the agrarian policy of Europe. As we have seen already, in recent years, the govern-

[1] Or prevents them from falling.

ments of Europe have erected higher and higher obstacles to the importation of agricultural products. Since the middle of the twenties, tariffs on agricultural imports have in some cases increased by several hundreds per cent. In Germany and Italy in particular, the duties have not only been such as to preserve from competition existing supplies, they have even called into being an additional volume of production. The effect of all this on the immediate prosperity of the world has been disastrous. The areas which have specialized on supplying these excluded products have been plunged into depression. Faced with severe exchange difficulties, they themselves have resorted to tariffs. The manufacturers of Europe have suffered accordingly. Even the payment of interest on debt in some cases has been suspended. The movement of new capital has diminished almost to zero. No one who has perused the relentless analysis by which Sir Frederick Leith Ross has established these facts can doubt the harmfulness of the impact effects of recent agrarian protectionism.[1]

But putting all this on one side as appertaining to the difficulties of the "transition", it must surely be obvious that the long-run effect must be to produce consequences which, from the inter-

[1] See Annex I to the Memorandum of the Economic Committee of the League of Nations, *Considerations on the Present Evolution of Agricultural Protectionism.*

national point of view, cannot be regarded as other than irrational. Even if the tremendous changes involved in reversing the trend of half a century could be carried through overnight, and the mobile resources of the world redistributed without friction in the lines of production appropriate to the new obstacles, it would surely be a mistake to do so. From the international point of view, there can be no justification for the production at high costs in Europe of agricultural products which could be produced at low costs in Australia and the Argentine, nor for the production in Australia and the Argentine at high cost of manufactures which could be produced at low costs in Europe. The thing is ridiculous. If it were not for the division of the surface of the earth into separate national areas it would not be thought of. Even in the most favourable conditions, the only possible gainers would be the owners of land and fixed resources in the protected industries. And if, as an indirect effect of these measures, protectionism abroad is increased, it is doubtful whether even these will benefit.

All this would probably be admitted by a majority of informed opinion nowadays. The evils of agrarian protectionism have become so conspicuous that their existence is not open to serious question. Today the intelligent apologists of such measures do so on avowedly political grounds, the desirability of safeguarding food supplies in time of war, the undesirability of falling foul of the rural electorate, the difficulty of breaking down the monopolistic obstacles which the rural labourer displaced by foreign competition might encounter in his search for employment. And so on. Mr. Walter Elliot and the landlords of East Prussia may continue to declaim the rustic argument that anything which puts money into the pockets of agriculturists is good for the world as a whole. But intellectually their position becomes less and less defensible.

But while the results of agricultural protection would be fairly generally judged to be bad, there is much more division of opinion about the protection of manufactures. It is often urged that the technique of manufacturing industry at the present day renders international division of labour much less advantageous than in the past. You can make almost anything anywhere nowadays, it is said. It does not much matter where your plant is located.

This sounds impressive. But it is really rather shallow. It may be true that it is physically possible to produce almost anything anywhere. But it does not follow at all that it is economical to do so. It is all a matter of costs. As we have seen, the advantage of international division of labour is *not* that it permits you to get from elsewhere only those products which you cannot produce at home, but rather that it permits you

CH. III SIGNIFICANCE OF NATIONAL PLANNING 51

to get from elsewhere all products in whose manufacture your costs of production are not lower than anywhere else. So long as the costs of production are different for different commodities in different areas, so long will it be advantageous for the inhabitants of each area to specialize in producing the things in which their costs of production are least and to procure the rest from elsewhere. Now these cost differences depend in the last resort on differences of the relative scarcities in different parts of the world of the different factors of production—depend, that is to say, on the existence of differences of efficiency wages, differences of rents, differences of raw material costs, transport charges and the like. There is really no presumption that such differences have ceased to exist with the coming of modern technical methods. Nor is there any presumption that the use of such methods renders any less essential nice attention to such matters. On the contrary, indeed, it is the first essential of the successful conduct of any kind of productive enterprise. Thread is produced on spindles ("manufacture") and butter is produced in churns ("agriculture"). But there is not one shade of difference between the two types of production as regards the relevance of costs and prices as indices of their most efficient location.

We can see this even more clearly if, for a

moment, we assume the contrary. If it really be true, as is asserted by the apologists for industrial protection, that the technique of modern manufacture makes the location of particular industries a matter of economic indifference, then it would follow immediately that there should be no real difficulty in establishing a manufacturing industry anywhere without the aid of a tariff. If it is really true that you can produce anything anywhere as economically as anywhere else, then it may well be asked why all this bother about protection? If the cost of production in any one part of the world is just as low as anywhere else, there should be no need of protective duties to make possible the existence of any type of industry deemed desirable.

But of course it is not so. In the absence of tariffs, the distribution of manufacturing industry between different areas would be very radically different. This is not a matter of conjecture. It is a proposition to which the most elementary facts of modern industry bear witness. How many of the branch factories which have been set up in different areas by the great international patent-holding companies to escape local tariffs would have come into being at all in the absence of such obstacles? Clearly very few. It needs a high tariff to bring them at all. And it needs a high tariff, too, to keep them prosperous once they have been established.

CH. III SIGNIFICANCE OF NATIONAL PLANNING 53

Confronted with facts of this sort, the advocate of industrial protection usually retreats upon the argument for large markets. Unless the market is secured by tariffs, it is said, the benefits of large-scale production can never fully be realized. The tariff eliminates the insecurity which is inimical to the development of large business. It is, as it were, the instrument of rationalization.

This is really the weakest position of all. To say at the present day that the multiplication of tariffs is conducive to the existence of wide and secure markets is so absurd a misreading of the facts that it scarcely seems necessary to spend time refuting it. It is of course conceivable that particular manufacturing units might run at less cost if a market were assured to them by a tariff, though we usually hear more of such arguments before the tariff is granted than when it has come into operation. But to concentrate upon this possibility to the neglect of the virtual certainties of a situation where there exist tariff-making powers on the part of a multiplicity of governments is surely to lose all perspective. For every case where the existence of tariffs has permitted such economies, there could be established many more where it prevents them coming into existence. Can it really be supposed that the economies of American mass production would be anything like so great if each of the forty-eight states of the Union were surrounded by a tariff ? Is it very sensible even to argue that these economies would be lost if the federal tariff itself were to be lowered ?

The fact is that, from the international point of view, planning by tariffs must necessarily be unsatisfactory, if only by reason of the complete unsuitability of the different areas of administration. It does not need much reflection to perceive that the nature of the existing tariff systems of the world is entirely contingent upon the accidental arrangement of the divisions over which the various sovereign states have authority. If the German Empire had not happened to include large manufacturing districts whose inhabitants could be made to pay the high prices necessary for the maintenance of the incomes of East Prussian landowners, there would have been no purpose in the erection of barriers to agricultural imports in that area—just as there would be very little purpose in the erection of barriers to the importation of coal into Great Britain. Some of the areas are large, such as Soviet Russia and the United States. Some are small, such as Belgium, New Zealand and the republics of Central America. But one and all have this common characteristic, that as units for the organization of production they have no relation to anything which is relevant to this purpose. They have been determined by wars, royal marriages, accidental geographical discovery and the haggling of politicians at conference tables—by almost anything, in short, but consideration of their suitability for the administration of economic resources. Whatever may be the validity of the arguments by which the desirability for this or that nation of fostering this or that industry may be established—and, as the classical free-trade argument has shown, most of these arguments are pretty fragile—from the international point of view the whole thing is absurd. It is conceivable that a world authority with perfect knowledge might in certain cases have occasion to interfere with the free working of private enterprise. But whether this is so or not, it is certain that the lines on which it would intervene would differ completely from the lines on which tariffs are planned by national governments. Rational world planning would attempt to extend the international division of labour. National planning by tariffs has the effect of restricting it.

4. What is true of planning by tariffs is true *a fortiori* of quantitative regulation—of quotas and licence systems. They involve a diminution of international trade, a wasteful utilization of world resources. And, as we have seen in recent years, they involve a dislocation of the mechanism of international exchange which is much more serious than that caused by any but the highest tariffs.

For, although the tariff is an impediment to trade, it need not be a prohibitive impediment. It imposes a toll upon incoming goods which makes it unprofitable to import them until the domestic price has reached a certain limit. But beyond that, if the tariff is not changed, the goods are admitted. If there are new changes in the conditions of supply and demand the volume of trade is automatically adopted. It is as though the obstacles to navigation were increased by the deposit of more rocks in the estuary. But provided it is worth while taking the extra trouble, the ships may still come in.

With the quota, however, it is different. So long as the quota is not changed, the volume of trade is definitely limited. No matter how great the willingness of the foreign producer to bear extra burdens, no matter how tempting the rise of prices in the home market, the volume of goods allowed to come in is fixed. The conditions of supply and demand may alter radically, but unless the quota is changed, no change in foreign importation is possible. It is as though the channels of navigation were closed by dams once a certain number of ships had gone through.

But cannot the quota be shifted? Quite obviously it can and often is. But the shifts are a cumbersome business and, as we shall see later on, they are productive of much friction and dislocation. Moreover, the probabilities are against

CH. III SIGNIFICANCE OF NATIONAL PLANNING 57

the shifts being made in what, from the international point of view, can be called the equilibrium direction. A quota is not likely to be enlarged if a change in productive conditions elsewhere makes it possible for the foreigner to offer his goods on cheaper terms. It will be enlarged only if domestic production fails so badly that the consumers will not stand the conditions of shortage or if trade negotiations make it necessary to enlarge particular quotas as part of a general bargain.[1] The British Pig Reorganization Commission, whose report is the *locus classicus* of the theory of quotas as instruments of long-term planning, definitely recommended that the total amount of bacon permitted to consumers should be fixed at the consumption of certain base years and that the import quota should fluctuate with fluctuations of domestic production. From the international point of view it is difficult to imagine a much more pernicious arrangement.

It follows, then, that a distribution of the productive forces of the world which, from the international point of view, can be regarded as satisfactory, is not likely to be fostered by quotas. The prospects are not improved if we imagine quantitative regulation of this sort to be supplanted by thoroughgoing state purchase. It is

---

[1] The connection between quotas and bilateral trade agreements will be more fully discussed in Part II, which deals with plans involving more than one government. See Chapter V, section 2.

true that if we suppose the import boards of a small state to be operating freely in a world otherwise given over to relatively free markets, we can conceive a certain elasticity of opportunity not available under the quota system. But such a conception cannot be generalized. If many countries set up import and export monopolies, then the competitive market disappears and, as we shall see later on, completely new problems emerge. In any case the tendency to protection is not likely to be reversed by such bodies. The advocates of the policy of import boards for the purchase of agricultural products for Great Britain have often urged their proposals on the ground that they would make possible a revival of British agriculture.[1] It is not easy to believe that an import monopoly would be permitted to behave so as to " jeopardize " domestic industry. On the contrary, it is probable that the tendency to support the *status quo* and to resist desirable change would be even stronger than under tariffs.

So far as imports are concerned, then, resort to more thoroughgoing forms of planning seems to offer no hope of escape from the toils of economic nationalism. The international division of labour is likely to be impaired even more than

[1] See for instance *An Alternative to Tariffs* (Political Quarterly, vol. II. pp. 186–203), the late Mr E. F. Wise. A comment on these proposals by the present author is to be found in the same volume, pp. 204–223.

it is under tariffs. Nor is the position likely to be improved by the granting of subsidies to export or by the creation of export monopolies which, by charging high prices to consumers at home, are enabled to raise much greater concealed subsidies for dumping abroad than could ever be procured from the Exchequer. On the contrary indeed. Quite apart from the increased rigidity and resistance to change which such a system almost necessarily introduces, the division of labour is likely to be still further distorted. There will be still more of the wrong industries in the wrong places.

For the fact is that neither export nor production for the home market are activities to be desired for their own sake. It is this elementary principle which the advocates of these types of planning seem incapable of grasping. It is one of the cardinal fallacies of contemporary policy that, wishing to provide the greatest income for the greatest number, it seeks to achieve this end by making the maintenance (or the increase) of particular lines of industry the chief objective of policy. But the greatest income, the greatest satisfaction of demand, is not to be secured by safeguarding or fostering industries which do not pay. No industry is sacrosanct as such. Only that policy maximizes the social income which leads to the continuous application of resources at the points of greatest productivity.

60 INDEPENDENT NATIONAL PLANNING PT. I

If under competitive conditions it does not pay to produce a commodity either for export or for home consumption, that is proof that this criterion is not satisfied. It is a proof that some at least of the factors of production can produce a more valuable product elsewhere. To maintain, by tariffs, by quotas, by subsidies, or by discriminating price-charging, industries menaced by foreign competition, either in domestic or in foreign markets, is a doubtful benefit, even from the national point of view. From the international point of view it can only be conceived as adding to the general confusion.

5. It is sometimes thought that these difficulties arise only because the different national plans are not sufficiently comprehensive. It is admitted that, when the state attempts to control the development of isolated parts of the national industry, its plans tend to be affected with sectionalism. But, if it assumes control of the entire field, it is said, this deficiency will be eliminated. It will then plan the system as a whole, shifting resources from one point to another as changes in the general conditions of supply and demand make it desirable to do so. While there is partial planning, the position is worse than it would be with no planning at all. But once planning has become general, this is all changed. The distribution of resources is even more in accordance

CH. III SIGNIFICANCE OF NATIONAL PLANNING 61

with the requirements of a rational international division of labour than it would be under a system of economic freedom.

If this were true, it would greatly clarify the issue. The only case for partial planning would be that it so aggravated the difficulties of the situation that it made complete national planning inevitable. But unfortunately the whole argument depends on a series of most improbable assumptions. And unless these assumptions are justified, there is reason to believe that the disadvantages of complete national planning are likely to be even greater than the disadvantages of less ambitious forms of control.

Let us look for a moment at the political mechanics of the system. The argument clearly assumes that the different national authorities have both the will and the power continually to adapt their arrangements to the requirements of the international division of labour. Now, whatever may be the case as regards their will, it is really very unlikely that they will have the power—at any rate so long as democratic conditions prevail. Under democratic conditions the members of the different industrial groups will feel that, in the last analysis, it is their representatives who determine the conditions of their employment. It is most unlikely that they will submit to be moved from place to place and from occupation to occupation if there seems an opportunity of preventing it by political action. We know by experience how difficult it is to induce people to change their occupation if there appears to be the remotest chance of their obtaining state support if they stay where they are. Under democratic conditions, even the shifting of a government dockyard encounters the most formidable resistance. If government control of industry becomes general, it is very difficult to believe that the probability of sectional resistance to change will not exert at least as powerful an influence on national planning as the desirability of employing resources at the point of maximum return. Indeed, so great are likely to be the obstacles presented even to what adaptation is thought to be absolutely essential, that a strong tendency to the supersession of democratic by dictatorial forms of organization is not at all improbable. It is no accident that, in the areas in which progress towards complete national planning is furthest advanced, political arrangements are least democratic.

But dictatorship too has its limits. The authorities of a totalitarian state will not wish to inconvenience their subjects by making them shift very often. They will not wish to multiply "unnecessary" causes of friction. For this reason they will be subject to strong temptation so to arrange their productive organization as to minimise outside contacts, even at the cost

CH. III SIGNIFICANCE OF NATIONAL PLANNING 63

of substantial sacrifice of real income. They will try to get all possible causes of change under their own control. This is clearly not the way to the most productive international division of labour. It is the way to the maximum of autarky compatible with the potentialities of the natural resources of the national areas concerned.

But let us ignore these political probabilities. Let us suppose that the planning authorities have a completely free hand to do what they like with the national resources. Even so, the assumption that they would dispose of these resources in such a way as to promote what, from the international point of view, would be the optimal forms of international co-operation, rests upon very weak foundations.

For the fact is that if production is controlled by extensive quasi-monopolistic units of this kind, the disposition of resources which seems most conducive to the advantage of the members of these units is not necessarily a distribution of resources which is in any sense optimal from the point of view of society as a whole. If a small state sets up trading monopolies in a world of otherwise competitive markets, it is improbable that its operations will very greatly affect the course of the markets in which it deals. If it follows the movements of the markets, it will be conforming to the requirements of the international optimum. The policy which maximizes its takings will contribute also to the maximization of world production, measured in price terms. But if it forms a large element in any of these markets, then contradictions arise. The interests of the group may be opposed to the interests of the rest of the world. The group may gain by restriction, the rest only by plenty. And if this method of organization becomes general, then further disharmonies are probable. The world market is frozen into a series of geographical monopolies : and its nature is completely transformed. There is no longer any reason to believe in the emergence of internationally harmonious arrangements. There is no price which is determinate apart from considerations of strategy. The result of the process of exchange is determined by a sort of political negotiation. There is no presumption at all that it conduces to anything which, from the international point of view, can be called a rational utilisation of resources. For the presumption that regulation of production according to the dictates of the market will be conducive to general harmony, is justified only when the units which deal are relatively small. There is no presumption whatever that the different national states form units which satisfy this criterion.

But, it may be asked, would not the organization of the different national areas on socialistic lines be merely a prelude to their amalgamation into a system of world socialism? Is not this perhaps another of those disagreeable transitions through which it is necessary to pass before reaching more satisfactory arrangements? It is this hope which inspires many socialists who urge local nationalization while still rendering lip-service to the international ideal.

It is not our intention at this stage to investigate the problem whether socialism on completely international lines would be a satisfactory solution of the problem of rational international planning. That will come up for extensive discussion later on.[1] But it is certainly germane to our present enquiry to observe that the organization of the world on national socialist lines is not necessarily a step in that direction. Indeed, it is almost certain to make the achievement of international socialism much more difficult than ever before.

For international socialism, whatever else it is, is essentially a state of affairs in which the resources of the different parts of the world are the property of the world as a whole. It is clearly incompatible with this that the resources in the different national areas should be owned by the national states. But, once the instruments of production have been nationalized, the obstacles to their internationalization are likely to be most formidable. For the value of the instruments

[1] See Part III, Chapter VIII, below.

of production in the different national areas varies greatly; and the real income per head, calculated on the assumption of collective ownership of these resources, varies greatly also. Some areas, such as Great Britain and the United States, are relatively rich. Others, such as Italy and Japan, are relatively poor. Let us suppose that complete socialization takes place within such areas and that the average incomes thus calculated become actual. Is there any reason to suppose that the citizens of the wealthier areas will be prepared to share the sources of their incomes with the citizens of the poorer? It is surely most improbable. It is difficult enough to get the inhabitants of local government areas where the value of rateable property is high to merge their rights of taxation with those of the inhabitants of areas where the value of rateable property is low. When it is a matter of pooling the total resources of different national units, the obstacles are likely to be so great as to be totally insurmountable—at any rate by peaceful methods. From the international point of view, national socialism involves the creation of forms of inequality which are likely to be more permanent and more productive of extensive friction than anything which arises in a regime of free enterprise and diffused ownership. There is no vested interest more intractable than the vested interests of national groups.

CH. III SIGNIFICANCE OF NATIONAL PLANNING 67

It is surprising that this has not been more widely recognized. For it has long been generally acknowledged that collective ownership of the instruments of production used in particular industries by the people who happen to work in these industries, is incompatible with the existence of a socialist order of society and is likely to impair its achievement. The incompatibility of socialism and industrial syndicalism is an ancient platitude.[1] But collective ownership of the instruments of production used in particular areas by the people who happen to live in those areas is on a precisely similar footing. "The mines for the miners" and "Papua for the Papuans" are analytically similar slogans. Industrial syndicalism and national socialism are highly symmetrical concepts. They are each incompatible with the realization of the international socialist ideal.

The contradiction has not altogether escaped notice. " Even national socialism, in most countries, is still remote," says Mr. Bertrand Russell, " but if once established it will make the next step more difficult, not less. Under capitalism, oil magnates are objects of envy, and a socialistic agitation against them is politically feasible. But when, as in Russia, the oil belongs to the national state, the whole nation is

[1] Witness the celebrated Fabian gibe, " The sewers for the sewage men ? "

interested in preventing its transfer to the world state. It will, therefore, be necessary to establish a firm military control by the international force before such a transfer can be effected. We are thus driven to the conclusion that internationalism must be established first in the military sphere, and only at a later stage extended to economic matters."[1]

Thus, whatever its merits from the national point of view, from the international point of view national socialism is a step in a backward direction.

6. We can see this even more clearly if we turn to the effects of independent national planning on the international distribution of new capital.

Under conditions of free investment, capital flows to the point of maximum return, account being taken of variations of risk. This means that capital tends to flow from areas where it is relatively plentiful to areas where it is relatively scarce. Now the different parts of the world are in very different stages of economic development. There is reason to suppose that, for a very long time to come, given peace, stable government and freedom of investment, capital would flow from those parts which are relatively rich to those parts which are relatively poor, with benefits to all

[1] *Which Way to Peace*, pp. 176-177.

concerned. From the economic point of view the world is still relatively undeveloped; and the prospects of increased wealth all round, which would follow better exploitation of its resources, are great.

But under national planning this process of development must inevitably be limited. This is not merely a matter of the immense obstacle to international investment which is offered by that form of national planning which involves instability of exchanges; it is also the effect of planning as regards long-term investment. So long as the governments of areas where capital is relatively scarce are unwilling to see domestic resources controlled by foreign owners; so long as the authorities of the areas where capital is relatively plentiful impose hindrances on its movement elsewhere—and, as we have seen, as national planning grows, this must come more and more to be the case—so long must this relative impoverishment of the world continue. There must be stagnation and ultra-cheap money in the centres which would have exported capital, financial stress and a chronic scarcity of capital in the centres which would have imported it. Moreover for a long time—and this is a point which especially concerns Great Britain—the great export trades of the capital exporting centres, which have been geared up, so to speak, to meet the demands created by a large export of capital, must remain depressed. Not merely the business of acceptance and new issue, but the whole business of export must suffer from the stoppage of free capital movement.

It may be said that all this is hasty generalization from the difficulties of the moment, and that "when things get better"—it is never stated quite how—even under the regime of separate national planning, we shall see a revival of orderly international borrowing and lending.

It is to be feared that the wish is father to the thought. For the probabilities are all in the other direction. The existence of national controls of the business of investment is likely to make the movement of capital not more, but very much less, than would otherwise be the case. When a set of investors in one country lends to another set of borrowers elsewhere, that is an affair of private business, in which the intervention of governments is the exception rather than the rule. But when the investment board of one country lends to the investment board of another, this is *ipso facto* a matter of high diplomacy involving political risks and considerations quite unconnected with the relative scarcity of capital in the areas concerned. It is really not to be expected that, under such a regime, the movement of capital for purely "productive" purposes would be on anything like the scale which might be expected in a regime of free private invest-

CH. III SIGNIFICANCE OF NATIONAL PLANNING 71

ment, or in anything like the same direction. The Russian credits are sometimes invoked as a demonstration that, even under national socialism, some borrowing takes place. But the example is very unconvincing. If the Revolution had taken a different form and there had been scope for free investment in Russia, can there really be any doubt that the volume of foreign investment in those parts since the war would have been incomparably greater? A world of separate national planning must be a world in which the undeveloped areas are developed much less rapidly and at much greater cost than would be the case in a world of international co-operation. And the centres which in the past have grown up to organize the business of international investment must be doomed either to decline or to a very radical transformation of their business.

7. As with the movement of capital so with the movement of people. In a world of free migration there would be a tendency for labour to move from the areas where productivity was relatively low to the areas where productivity was relatively high. In so far as it was desired to make world production a maximum, this would obviously be rational. In a world state, it would be absurd to apply much labour at points of low productivity in some parts and little labour at points of high productivity in others. We need

not enquire here whether, in such a state, from every point of view, complete freedom of migration would be desirable. There will be more to say about that later on. But obviously the present state of affairs, with congestion in some parts and vast unoccupied spaces in others, would be regarded as quite ridiculous.

In a world of national planning, as we have seen, migration is likely to be reduced to a minimum. The shifting of humanity, which, if it has never been completely free, has at least been almost continuous since the beginning of history, will be suspended or greatly retarded. With the present distribution of labour this will mean a considerable sacrifice. Moreover, if present tendencies of net survival rates continue, the distribution will become more and more anomalous. The low reproduction-rate areas, which, broadly speaking, are more richly endowed with natural and artificial resources, will become less populated. The high reproduction-rate areas will become even more overcrowded. Indeed, taking a long view it is fairly certain that such a situation could not persist. Sooner or later the more fertile peoples, or at least the more vigorous among them, would burst the barriers which hemmed them in and enter into what they regarded as their rightful domain. But this would be a very different business from the gradual redistribution which would take place in the absence of national

CH. III SIGNIFICANCE OF NATIONAL PLANNING 73

barriers; and much more than the obstacles to migration might easily be destroyed in the process.

This brings us to matters which may more conveniently be treated in the next chapter.

CHAPTER IV

NATIONAL PLANNING AND INTERNATIONAL STABILITY

1. It was one of the conclusions of the last chapter that independent national planning tends to a diminution of international trade. However much it may be attempted to offset this tendency by resort to export subsidies and dumping, there seems strong reason to suppose that independent attempts to plan economic activities *within* national areas must lead to a diminution of economic relations *between* national areas. Consciously or not, national planning has a strong autarkistic bias.

If this tendency were to be carried to its logical conclusion, the analysis of the last chapter would be sufficient to enable us to judge its implications. The benefits of international co-operation would be sacrificed. Division of labour, the economies of mass production, would be limited to national areas. It would be as though there had been a fragmentation of the planet along the lines of division of the political maps.

The inhabitants of each fragment would be deprived of resort to outside supplies. The co-existence of other inhabited fragments would be irrelevant from the economic point of view. The world as a whole would be poorer than it might be with international co-operation.

Such extreme developments are not likely. The apparatus of modern life is so dependent on supplies of raw materials, unequally distributed between the different national areas, that it is most improbable that the inhabitants of the majority of such areas would be content with the very drastic alterations of their habits which abstention from the consumption of all commodities containing imported ingredients would involve. Even the Russians, with their vast variety of resources and their determination to have everything possible under central control, are anxious to import certain classes of commodities. Moreover, the countries which are especially dependent on the export of such materials would certainly make strong efforts to secure outlets, even at some sacrifice of protection for domestic manufacture. The net effect of the very drastic economic nationalism which seems to lie ahead is likely to be a severe curtailment, rather than a total cessation, of international business. There will still be some foreign trade.

Now to judge such a state of affairs, it is not sufficient to analyse its relation to an ideal international division of labour. It is necessary also to ascertain how it would work as a going system. We have to enquire concerning the nature of the international connections remaining, how they would change, how these changes would affect internal economic conditions, how they would affect international political relations. It is sometimes claimed that, although national planning involves a sacrifice of the wealth which would accrue from a greater international division of labour, yet the gain in stability which is involved by the greater control of the local states over economic conditions within their jurisdiction is such as to make the sacrifice worth while. This claim must be seriously examined.

2. Let us commence by examining international markets under conditions of widespread national planning. It is quite possible, of course, that different national areas may attempt to enter into specially intimate relations with other areas in order to mitigate some of the disadvantages of complete isolation. In fact, we shall see, as the argument proceeds, that this is a very probable development. For the moment, however, since we are attempting to see the consequences of completely independent planning, let us leave this possibility out of account. Let us assume that the different national authorities set up import and export boards to deal in the

CH. IV INTERNATIONAL STABILITY

various commodities in which they are interested; and let us assume that these different boards are not tied by long-term contracts to the boards of other areas.

Such arrangements, as we have seen, are obviously far from constituting a system of competitive markets. There are no middlemen. The units which deal are few and they are large. Indeed the object of national planning in this sphere is avowedly the elimination of free markets with their "wasteful" competition and their "parasitical" middlemen. There will be dealing. But it will be skies apart from the dealing of pre-interventionist days. As we have seen, it will be the dealing, not of a system of economic freedom, but the dealing of a system of geographical syndicalism.

Now we have seen already that this involves much greater obstacles to what, from the international point of view, is to be regarded as a satisfactory distribution of resources. But it means too a much greater instability of prices. So long as the different trading bodies remain free—and this is the assumption we are making—the fluctuation of prices is likely to be wider and more discontinuous than in markets which are more competitive. This is abundantly borne out by actual experience. It is well known that when the market for any particular commodity is dominated by a few large concerns, then, unless there are agreements between them, the fluctuations are large and discontinuous. Moreover, it must be remembered that the actions of the various boards are likely to be much more the instruments of political strategy, much less dictated by considerations of profit, than the actions of private dealers. A change in internal policy, the alteration of a ministry, a decision to carry through this or that spectacular move to satisfy or impress public opinion — these are matters which would influence world prices under independent national planning much more than under free capitalism. The whole history of government dealing proves this. The dealings of the Federal Farm Board are apt examples of tendencies which national planning might well make general.

Such conditions would involve certain sacrifices. Under competitive conditions the world market acts as a sort of damping mechanism. The disturbing effects of local gluts and shortages are absorbed and spread over a much wider area. If home production fails, then additional supplies can be procured from abroad without a great rise of prices. If home production is unexpectedly bountiful, then it can be unloaded without much fall. The probability of world glut or world shortage is obviously much less than the probability of glut or shortage in particular areas.

Now the syndicalization of the market would

CH. IV   INTERNATIONAL STABILITY   79

impair this very mechanism. The fact that the units of dealing were so large would indeed tend to bring into play a directly contrary tendency. The various boards would tend to market manœuvres which might easily cause oscillations rather than tend to damp them down. Consider for instance the effects of an unexpectedly plentiful harvest in one particular area. It would obviously be impossible for the export board of that area to market it all in the usual time without some cut in price. But it is under no compulsion to do so. It may accumulate stocks and wait. If it is lucky, the turn of the market may save it. But if not, then the stocks accumulate more and more, prices are depressed still further and the disturbance all round will be greater than if dealing had been continuous. The experience of the Canadian wheat pool affords abundant examples of such disturbances.

Such instability of the market will present certain new problems for the organization of production. The organizers of domestic industry concerned with the foreign market will be unable to plan ahead with anything like the certainty which they will desire. Their plans will be liable to be disorganized by sudden and discontinuous changes. The relative profitability of different lines of production will fluctuate more than under competitive capitalism.

For all these reasons there is a very strong

probability that the state of affairs we have been assuming, a state of completely free dealing between the various trading bodies, will be the exception rather than the rule. Faced with the chaos of syndicalistic dealing, the different states will each seek to enter into special arrangements with others with whom they are able to strike advantageous bargains. Free dealing will give way to bilateral agreements. Again this is not a purely speculative conjecture. Under capitalism, when, owing to the prevalence of monopoly, there is great uncertainty with regard to supplies and markets, there is a tendency to similar arrangements, businesses seeking to assure their supplies by amalgamation with other businesses at different stages of production. The difference is that, under capitalism, such arrangements are less likely to be lasting. In the absence of special technical conditions involving special technical advantage in vertical integration, the advantages of buying in the cheapest and selling in the dearest market continually tend to the disruption of permanent arrangements of this kind.

3. But let us defer such considerations until the second part of this essay where we shall be considering deliberate interstate planning in a more systematic manner. Let us for the present retain the assumption of independent national planning and let us extend our examination of its

implications to the wider effects of change in the fundamental conditions of production.

It follows from what has been said already that it is improbable that the various national systems will be especially adaptable to change. The tariff is an instrument of resistance quite as much as an instrument of construction. And experience does not suggest that, when the state has sunk capital in particular lines of enterprise, it will show any remarkable alacrity in writing it off as a loss if conditions change to its disadvantage. The whole literature of contemporary planning abounds in complaints that, under a free system, plant must be abandoned before it is physically worn out, that railways must be left unused although they are still capable of providing transport, and so on. One of the advantages of planning, it is claimed, is that it will eliminate all this. The rate of physical depreciation will set the pace of change. Moreover, under democracy at any rate, there are notorious obstacles to rapid adaptation of government arrangements. It is not easy to close down an army barracks if the local M.P. is an influential person. To change the location of whole branches of manufacturing industry might be politically very difficult.

But none the less, it is not possible to think change out of the picture. Quite apart from the temporary fluctuations of harvests and animal husbandry, there will be changes in population, changes in availability of mineral resources, changes in capital supply, changes in technical knowledge, changes in consumers' demand. In a world in which these changes take place at a different pace in different places, their incidence on the different national systems is bound to be such as to call for adaptation.

Let us try to trace the probable effects of some of these changes. Let us suppose, for instance, a technical discovery making it possible for the inhabitants of a certain area to produce certain commodities much more cheaply than heretofore and much more cheaply than their competitors in other countries — an agricultural invention making possible the production of wheat on soils which had hitherto no productive uses might be a case in point.

Under a free system, the cheaper commodities would at once be accepted in the general world market. The increase in supply would lead to a fall in prices. The real incomes of consumers would rise. Those enterprises elsewhere, whose costs of production were such that they could only continue on a profitable basis at a higher price, would contract, and the mobile resources employed here would be devoted to other types of production for which previously they could not be spared. If the change were such as substantially to alter relative rates of remuneration in the different national areas, there would be some migration from the area where relative rates had fallen to the area where relative rates had risen. In the end, all the members of the world community would have their real incomes increased to the extent that the new invention made possible—save the owners of fixed resources in the high cost areas, who might suffer a permanent fall. This is not an imaginary picture. Broadly speaking, it is an outline of the main effects of the opening-up of new areas of agricultural production in the second half of the nineteenth century.

Under independent national planning, however, the effects would be radically different. It is possible of course that, subject to the difficulties of the imperfect world market which we have noticed above, the various states would accept the cheap imports and attempt to adjust their organization to something like the free-trade optimum. But how improbable this is! What vast resistances such a change would encounter! "Never must we allow (British, American, German) agriculture to be exterminated by cheap foreign imports", it would be said. "These products of cheap soils must not injure the value of state property." "The interest of the consumer must not be allowed to impair the proper balance of our national system." Such pleas sound very familiar. They are the standard clichés of the political propaganda of our day.

Is it really at all plausible to argue that under a system in which there was still more planning it would all be different? Surely it is probable that the cheaper imports would be excluded, or at best that they would only be admitted in very limited doses.

But if this were so, it would mean that the realized, as distinct from the potential, benefits of the new knowledge would be greatly curtailed. If the exclusion were complete, then they would be confined entirely to the area in which the changes originated. And within this area the benefit would not be as great as under free conditions. For, shut out from the foreign markets, the inhabitants of that area would have to use the resources set free by the increase of productivity in producing other products at costs higher than need have been the case if they could have procured them from elsewhere by exchange. It would not be profitable for them to produce so much of the commodity whose cost of production had been cheapened. Again this is not a fanciful picture. It is a broad recapitulation of the effects of increases of agricultural productivity under the economic nationalism of the post-war period.

But this is not all. So far we have considered the effects of change in one area, in conditions in which the results of policy were merely such as to deprive all other areas of its benefits. The nations who exclude cheaper food in order to preserve the *status quo* in domestic agriculture are not necessarily absolutely poorer than before; they are merely not so much richer as they might have been had they accepted the fruits of increased productivity elsewhere. But the incidence of change is not always thus. And the effects of national planning may not be merely a curtailment of the benefits of technical progress: they may be an inability to escape from the otherwise transitional difficulties which that progress may occasion.

Let us consider the genesis of such a situation. Let us suppose an invention which results in a curtailment of demand for the staple article of export of a single state or small group of states. Suppose for example a change in methods of producing paper which while reducing the cost of production (and thus potentially benefiting world consumers) involves a considerable diminution in the demand for certain kinds of soft-wood timber. Or suppose some chemical discovery superseding the demand for some natural fertilizer, hitherto the main export of a small state.

In any case there would be transitional difficulties. The incidence of change is, by hypothesis, *in export markets*. It cannot be avoided by tariffs or such-like obstacles. In any case there would be some lowering of the value of land in the areas affected. Unless some of the population were willing to migrate, the equilibrium rate of wages would tend to be lowered too. Wages —in the last analysis real wages—would have to fall or there would be increased unemployment.

In a world of economic freedom, however, things would not end at this point. If migration were free, there would be emigration to areas where the value of the product of labour was higher. This would go on until the tendency to a fall in the rate of wages was arrested. There would be a redistribution of world population corresponding to the new conditions of supply and demand. Even if migration were not free, it would be possible for the inhabitants of the affected area to turn to other forms of production made profitable by the fall in the value of the local factors of production. It might well be that a slight fall of wages would attract capital from elsewhere to take advantage of the new conditions of production. And in this way, though all the ill effects of the change of demand might not be avoided, at least some of them would be. The producers originally affected would at least be better off than if they had been confined to their original occupation.

But in a world of economic nationalism how much harder would be the transition. There would be no outlet by way of migration : as we have seen, national planning precludes free migration. And the outlets for the new form of production to which the inhabitants of the affected areas might turn their hands would be limited greatly by the protectionism of national planning elsewhere. The "ruinous" competition of producers in the impoverished area would be resisted. In the few markets to which they succeeded in gaining access the lowering of price necessary to unload the increased supplies would be much greater than would be the case if the area of sale were less circumscribed. If the original falling-off of demand were very great, it might well be that the impoverishment of the inhabitants of the affected area would be catastrophic.

The picture is alarming. But it is not wholly imaginary. If we reflect on the recent history of the world it is not difficult to find examples. The causes of the increase of Japanese competition in recent years are many and complex. But one at least of these causes was the falling-off of demand for Japanese silk in American markets which followed the collapse of 1929. And one cause at least for the great severity of Japanese competition in the countries to which the Japanese goods have access is the very considerable obstacles which have been erected to the importation of such goods elsewhere. No doubt there is more in it than this. But the example is conducive to reflection ; and, as we shall see later, it has a further moral which is even more disturbing.

Now of course the larger the state and the wider the range of the natural resources within its boundaries, the smaller the probability of big changes in real incomes due to changes of this nature. Assuming that there is still free migration within their borders, national units of the size of the United States of America would not have much to fear on this score. The export market in one product might be hit. But there should be a sufficient range of alternative demands at home to prevent a serious absolute lowering of the average real income. It is the smaller countries and the countries more dependent on export which have most to fear from change in a world of national planning.

But none the less it is a mistake to think of the kind of difficulty now under discussion as arising only in connection with changes, such as changes in demand for, say, English coal or Cuban sugar. The case is really more far-reaching than that. The absence of facilities for migration may be the cause of considerable difficulties, even when it is a question, not of competing exports in foreign markets, but of competing imports in the home market. For in some cases it may be much easier for the labour displaced by cheap imports to be reabsorbed by migration to other national areas than by switching over to other forms of production at home. If migration is blocked by national planning, and if, as is notoriously the case in present conditions, the degree of national planning at home is such as to present stiff barriers to internal migration, the incidence of change on the producers affected may be prolonged and severe.

Again an example is not far to seek. In the nineteenth century, as the New World was opened up by the steamship and the railway, and as its agricultural products came in competition with the agricultural products of Europe, it was often easier, under the conditions then prevailing, for European agricultural labourers to migrate to similar occupations abroad, rather than to change their occupations completely within the national area in which they were then living. Great areas of the New World were populated in this way; and the social difficulties of the Old World were greatly eased in consequence. In the post-war period, with its almost universal obstacles to migration, this way of readjustment has been closed. At the same time, within the national areas, the increase of monopolistic obstacles fostered by national policy has made the internal system much more rigid. The result is that the acceleration of agricultural productivity elsewhere has produced in many cases a situation of great hardship for the agricultural producers of Europe. The various governments, unwilling to take steps to increase domestic mobility but distracted by the prospect of agrarian discontent, resort to tariffs and quotas, with the results we have already examined.[1] Thus the absence of freedom to migrate reinforces protectionist tendencies and produces a situation which will aggravate the political and economic instability of the world for many years to come. If there had been more freedom of migration in the post-war period, very many of our most insistent problems would have been eased.

4. If the analysis of the preceding sections is correct, it seems as if the policy of independent national planning were likely to lose the substance for the shadow, even in regard to stability. If the policy is generally adopted—and it is the most astounding naïveté to argue as if it could be restricted only to one's own national area—then instability is increased. It is not a question of bartering the prospects of greater wealth for greater security; security goes as well.

All this relates only to the economic consequences of independent national planning. Even more important and even more disturbing are its probable political consequences. There is reason to believe it is likely considerably to enhance international political friction. The idea that the peace of the world is likely to be safer if

[1] It is interesting to observe that the slowing-up of migration into the United States produced a flow of capital to Europe which otherwise would not have been likely to have arisen on anything like the same scale.

we " try to keep ourselves to ourselves " is not merely a pathetic fallacy, it is a highly dangerous delusion. We have already had occasion to note how national planning tends to what may be called—to borrow a very ugly word from a people who have carried this thing further than most—the politicalization (*Politizierung*) of international economic relations. The lending and borrowing of capital, in so far as it takes place at all, is a matter of high diplomacy. If experience of the past is any guide, it is likely to be much more dictated by consideration of political advantage than by calculations of economic gain : and the arrangement (or refusal) of such transactions is itself likely to be accompanied by much political friction. Even the everyday business of trade becomes a matter of international politics. Instead of the consignment of sardines from Utopia to Ruritania being a transaction between Utopian and Ruritanian merchants subject to the sanctions and penalties of the laws of their respective countries, it is a transaction between the representatives of sovereign states, subject only to the nebulous precepts of a sanctionless international law. The High Contracting Parties undertake to deliver and receive Sardines ! Obviously, if anything goes wrong, it is much more likely to lead to political friction than when private merchants are the parties involved.

Moreover, the very fact that dealing is undertaken by such large trading units as the agents of political states must introduce market complications which themselves are likely to lead to friction. The policies of the different boards themselves affect the course of the market. The prices fixed must depend on the actions of national representatives. This may very easily lead to suspicions and enmities which would not exist in a non-political market.

Again, actual examples are not difficult to discover. It is not possible to deny the political tension which was caused by the Russian incursions into the timber market. Dumping in general, which is made possible by state policy in regard to tariffs, is a notorious cause of international unfriendliness. The British Rubber Restriction went far to imperil our good relations with the United States of America. It does not need much imagination to conceive the resentment which would be caused in the southern states of the Union, if a British Cotton Import Board were depressing the price of cotton. It is only those who are blind because they do not want to see who can really deny that an increase of interstate trading involves a multiplication of opportunities for interstate friction.

5. But the " politicalization " of trade is not the only, or indeed the chief, political danger of

independent national planning. The main danger is the worsening of relations between states of unequal resources and populations—the " haves " and " have-nots " of popular discussion—which it almost certainly involves.

It is a commonplace of elementary economics that *so long as trade and migration are free*, from the economic point of view, the area of political jurisdiction is a matter of secondary importance. So long as political administration involves no discrimination against the foreigner, the fact of territorial possession involves no major gain, its absence no important disadvantage. This is by no means to deny all economic functions to governmental bodies: as we shall see later on, under pure liberalism as under pure collectivism they have most important and indispensable functions. Nor is it to deny the existence of a very real problem of the regional division of political administration: on a certain plane the problem of the most appropriate division of local government authorities has considerable economic significance. But speaking broadly, in a world perspective, it is true to say that, so long as trade and movement are free, the fact of territorial possession is a matter of secondary importance to the real incomes of the inhabitants of particular areas. We can imagine important disputes about rates or expenditure on drainage between the electors of different county councils.

But in the main the adult inhabitant of, shall we say, the county of Buckinghamshire cannot feel seriously aggrieved that the county of Oxfordshire is not " possessed " by his county council. To identify wide territorial jurisdiction with high wealth per head for the economic subjects is to commit the fundamental error of confusing territorial jurisdiction with property rights. It is true that this is very often done. It is one of the standard propagandist weapons of political nationalism. But it is an error nevertheless. If I am free to trade with people who live elsewhere, if I may invest money in enterprises in that region, if I may pack up my goods and chattels and transfer myself and my family to that locality and receive equal treatment under the law, then the fact that it is " owned " by another nation is a matter of minor importance so far as my real income is concerned. I may attach mystical significance to membership of a certain political community. I may believe that it is important that men of the same " blood " or political tradition should enjoy a common government. But so long as governmental divisions do not involve interference with the free movement of men, of capital or goods, these are " political " rather than "economic" matters.

But, once the principles of independent national planning hold sway, the position is changed completely. Once national areas are treated as if they were the private property of the state, their markets preserved for its citizens only, their resources open to development only by national labour and national capital, then territorial possession does matter very much indeed. If the depressed area of South Wales were a separate national area and if the citizens of that area were deprived of the opportunity of seeking work in more prosperous parts of Great Britain, the fact that the state of South Wales was so limited in area would be a very grave disadvantage. It would be a still greater disadvantage if, by reason of a desire to help, let us say, some depressed coalfield within the English frontier, they were prevented from selling any coal to English consumers. In such circumstances the absence of wider territorial possessions matters very much indeed. The claim for a place in the sun ceases to be empty bombast. It becomes the fateful expression of an urgent and insistent need.

Now this is a very serious matter—and the more fortunate a nation in its actual possessions, the more probable the eventual menace to its security. If it can justly be said by the leaders of a hungry people, " *Your* poverty is the result of *their* policy. *Your* deprivation is the result of *their* possession "—then there is grave risk of war. There is real danger of a combination of the " have-nots " to plunder the " haves ". It is often said that in modern times the origins of war have been chiefly economic. But this is not true. Examination of the facts does not bear it out. The idea of the leaders of national states being goaded on to war by grasping capitalists has scant counterpart in the recent past.[1] It has happened occasionally ; but in the majority of cases the causation of war has been exactly the reverse. Timid capitalists have been goaded into foreign investment to further the policy of diplomatic manœuvre. But in the near future the idea of the less fortunate peoples being provoked to predatory war by the exclusiveness of the more fortunate is likely to be a grim and terrible reality. In a liberal world the theory that the main causes of war are economic is a malignant invention. Independent national planning creates the conditions which make it true.

[1] Professor Staley's *War and the Private Investor* should be consulted by those who have any doubts on this subject. This masterly and dispassionate study has not yet received the attention it deserves.

PART II

PARTIAL INTERNATIONAL PLANNING

CHAPTER V

TRADE AGREEMENTS AND REGIONAL GROUPING

1. In the last three chapters we have been discussing the implications of independent national planning. We have traced the genesis of the various kinds of national planning now in vogue. We have seen that they involve at once a shrinkage of international division of labour and an increase of international instability. We have seen also that they involve an increase of the danger of war.

These tendencies are very actual. At the present day they are becoming obvious even to wide circles of the lay public. Trade has decreased. Conditions are more unstable. The shadow of war dominates everything. It is not unnatural, therefore, that, in such circumstances, men's minds should turn to the possibilities of wider kinds of planning, to the possibilities of interstate arrangements which should eliminate the dangers of planning on a purely national scale. It is to projects of this sort that we must now turn our attention. In this part of the essay we shall examine projects for international plans of a limited or partial character; in the next, international planning on a more comprehensive scale.

2. The simplest form of interstate planning is the bilateral trade agreement. In return for concessions as regards its own trade, each party to the agreement grants concessions to the other. Denmark agrees to take more British goods if Britain agrees not to exclude so many Danish goods. " Buy from those who buy from you " is the principle of their policy. In recent years very many such agreements have been negotiated.

Now bilateralism is not new. It is perhaps an exaggeration to say that it was a settled principle of policy in the early mercantilistic era. The " balance of bargains " system has had a more coherent existence in the minds of economic historians than in the pamphlets of the sixteenth and seventeenth centuries.[1] But the idea that to secure a satisfactory general balance of trade it was necessary to watch the balance with particular countries did influence both the thought and the practice of those times. The balance of trade with India was the subject of extensive controversy. At a later stage the balance of trade with France gave rise to some misgiving. From time to time, both dealings in foreign money and

[1] See Viner, " English Theories of Foreign Trade before Adam Smith," *Journal of Political Economy*, vol. 38, pp. 259-260.

the actual movements of goods were regulated with a view to bilateral balancing.

But as trade developed and insight into its ramifications became more general, such concern with particular balances became more and more exceptional. It was realized that triangular or multilateral trade was as natural for countries as for persons, and that many of the commercial developments which were thought to be most profitable would not have come into being if trade were regulated on strictly bilateral lines.[1] By the middle of the nineteenth century, it had become customary to enter into agreements whereby any reduction in obstacles to trade made to one government were automatically extended to all the others. The "most-favoured-nation clause", as such provisions were entitled, was the direct antithesis of the principle of bilateralism. And even up to the outbreak of the Great Depression, in spite of the prevalence of projects for preference systems and regional groupings, no frontal attack was made on the principles of multilateral trade.

Such a state of affairs, however, was incom-

---

[1] See, for instance, Adam Smith's trenchant comment on doctrines, whereby "The sneaking arts of underling tradesmen are erected into political maxims for the conduct of a great empire; for it is the most underling tradesmen only who make it a rule to employ chiefly their own customers. A great trader purchases his goods always where they are cheapest and best, without regard to any little interest of this kind." *The Wealth of Nations* (Cannan's Edition), vol. i, p. 457.

patible with the development of the tendencies which we have already examined. The resort to quantitative regulation of trade involves almost inevitably a reversion to bilateralism. The allotment of quotas involves separate bargaining with the different sources of imports. The destruction of the world markets makes resort to special agreements regarding " indispensable " supplies a strong probability.[1] Moreover, the various monetary controls, which have been so conspicuous a feature of recent crisis policy, make bilateral arrangements regarding trade almost indispensable. Arrangements to clear debts to a particular country against debts from that country involve stringent measures to bring the trade relationships concerned into some sort of equilibrium, if the clearing is not to break down. In the scramble for markets which has followed the spread of the now almost universal restrictionism, absence of discrimination between different customers has not seemed an important object of policy.

3. It is easy to understand all this as a desperate expedient of economic nationalism in difficulties. But it is not easy to regard it as a stage in the development of rational world planning. It is certainly less impracticable than complete isolationism. But, as compared with looser types

[1] See above, Chapter IV, para. 3.

of independent national planning, its advantages are not so obvious. It is probably easier to work. But it is doubtful whether it involves less disturbance to the international division of labour. And there are certain contradictions in the very idea of bilateralism which independent national planning need not necessarily involve.

If the world were divided into two national areas, it is obvious that, in equilibrium, payments out and payments in must exactly equal each other. If the inhabitants of one area were indebted to the inhabitants of the other area, there would not be equality between imports and exports, in the narrow sense of services currently rendered. The creditor country would have an excess of imports and the debtor country an excess of exports. But current claims and debts must completely cancel out. Indeed, we must take it as axiomatic that, in equilibrium, the payments between *any* group of individuals and the rest of the world must exactly balance. If it were not so, there would not be equilibrium.

But as soon as we assume that the world is divided into more than two areas, then, so long as trade is free, it does not in the least follow that there must be equality in this sense between the debts and claims of the inhabitants of any two groups taken separately. Indeed it is obvious that, if it were so, it would be a sheer fluke, a statistical accident for the silly season. It is indeed necessary that purchases from *all* groups taken together should balance sales to *all* groups taken together, if indebtedness is not to increase or capital to run down. If this does not happen there are forces tending to bring it about. But it is not in the least necessary that purchases from *each* group should balance sales to *each* group. There is no force operative which would tend to bring it about. It would be improbable if there were only three groups; and the greater the number of groups the more improbable it becomes. If a single individual told us that his sales to his several tradespeople exactly balanced their respective sales to him, we should scarcely credit his story. If trade were naturally bilateral, then money would be unnecessary.

It follows, therefore, that if attempts are made to force international trade into bilateral channels, much potential wealth must be sacrificed. International bilateralism is essentially a return to international barter. And just as a return to barter in general would restrict the general division of labour to those limits within which individual producers could find a direct coincidence of individual wants, so a return to barter in international transactions must restrict international division of labour to those limits which are set by the coincidence of international wants. The accident of the political subdivision of the world would impose completely arbitrary restrictions on what, from the international point of view, would be the most economical use of resources.

We can see this very clearly if we consider the effects of change in such a system. Let us suppose that at the outset the statistical fluke contemplated above had actually happened; that is to say that the general conditions of supply and demand were such that, not only did the payments between each area and all other areas together exactly balance, but that the payments between each area and each of the others taken separately also balanced exactly. In other words, let us suppose that the international division of labour which made costs a minimum also happened to be that which produced equality of bilateral balances.

Now let us suppose some simple change in the conditions of production. Let us suppose, for instance, the discovery of rare mineral resources in, let us say, Liberia. In order that bilateral balancing might continue, it would be necessary that the expansion of demand for this product in each country should be accompanied by an exactly parallel expansion of demand for the products of these countries in Liberia. If it were not so, then the " equilibrium " would be ruptured. And if it were attempted to maintain it by trade restrictions, then some, at least, of the benefits of the new discovery would be lost.

Suppose, for instance, there were an extensive

demand for this product in Great Britain. It is not at all certain that there would arise a corresponding demand in Liberia for British products. But under free conditions this would not matter. The Liberians might spend the proceeds of sales to inhabitants of Great Britain on products from elsewhere. But the people from whom they bought might be willing to buy British products. Or if they were not, then the people from whom they bought . . . and so on. It is not certain that equilibrium would be re-established without some readjustments of prices and costs at different points in the circle. But in principle there need be no more difficulty than when the lawyer buys more from the fruiterer without first having ascertained that that tradesman is likely to increase his demand for litigation.

But under bilateralism, these easy arrangements would be excluded. If the Liberian demand did not expand *pari passu* with the British, then the British import of Liberian products would be restricted. Thus the Liberian production would be prevented from expanding so far as would otherwise be profitable. And the British consumer would go unsatisfied. And the people elsewhere who would willingly have taken more British products but whose own products were more acceptable to Liberia, would be out of it altogether.

Now, no doubt, quantitatively considered, a

single set of losses of this kind may not be very great in relation to the sum-total of trade. But the cumulative effect of permanent prevention of other than bilateral expansion may be very great indeed. If every time that there occur changes in the general conditions of supply and demand, these changes are only allowed to work within the Procrustean limits of bilateral trade agreements, the retardation of the speed of economic development will be very considerable and the sacrifice of potential wealth will be great. Over short periods, indeed, it is probable that the optimal distribution of trade between different countries does not vary a great deal. But over longer periods it may be completely transformed. At any moment the magnitude of desirable change may be so small that to prevent it may seem a very minor evil. But, in the long run, it is just these small changes which amount to those big changes which we recognize as economic progress. The world would be a very much poorer place today if bilateralism had been the rule during the century that has just passed. And there does not seem any very convincing reason for believing that it will not be very much poorer than it might be, if bilateralism is to be the rule in the century that is to come. It is really very weak to argue that whereas the world was not ripe for bilateralism then, it is ripe for bilateralism now. For the world can only be ripe for bilateralism when it has been decided that production at high cost is more sensible than production at low cost; that is to say, when it has been decided that less wealth is to be preferred to more. Bilateralism is the negation of the main principle of productive economy.

4. The case against bilateralism is not limited to these rather statical conclusions. If the net effect of bilateralism were merely to arrest the speed of economic progress, then although the world as a whole is still very poor, it might be urged that the loss in potential wealth would be outweighed by a gain in stability of conditions. Better a limited division of labour and certainty, it might be said, than an unlimited division and uncertainty.

Unfortunately there is no reason to believe in the probability of such compensating advantages. If hitherto there had been no international trade, if the planning of international trade merely involved the setting of limits to trade relations which were yet to grow, then it is not inconceivable that the effects of bilateral restrictions might exhaust themselves in a limitation of wealth yet to be achieved. There would not be complete fragmentation of the planet as under thoroughgoing autarky. The international division of labour would exist. But it would be limited to the possibilities of direct barter.

But it is not so. As things are, bilateralism must be imposed on a world many parts of which have already become specialized to trade which is not bilateral. The *entrepôt* trade, the business of the great ports and commercial centres, depends upon trade relations which are essentially multilateral. If trade is to become bilateral these centres must decline. The industrial capital which has been invested in developments dependent on the possibility of triangular trade must be written off, and the labour which has become specialized in these centres and occupations must turn elsewhere for a living. The magnitude of the difficulties in centres such as Liverpool, Amsterdam, Hamburg, which must follow the suppression of multilateral trade is not easy to exaggerate.

But this is not all. There is no reason to believe that, even with these sacrifices, a world moving towards bilateralism would settle down into equilibrium. Bilateralism destroys the world market. It makes what trade is permitted a pure business of horse trading. And since, bilateralism or no bilateralism, the conditions of production and demand are continually changing, there is no reason to suppose that this business can reach any sort of stable conclusion. The trade connections of one country with another may be ruthlessly set aside overnight in order that the second country may be in a better position to bargain with a third. The execution of bargains which have been made involves the imposition of controls which themselves react on the volume of trade and in turn necessitate further bargains. So far from establishing a tendency towards greater stability and equilibrium, bilateralism seems to tend towards cumulative instability.

These conclusions are not "merely" theoretical. It is possible, indeed, that they may be reached by elementary reflections on the very nature of trade. It is not necessary to throw spanners into complex machinery to show that such a habit is productive of frictions. But in fact they are abundantly verified by experience. The spanners have actually been thrown and parts of the machine are jamming before our eyes. The decline in triangular transactions is one of the most conspicuous features of the present depression of international trade. The causes of this decline are various. In part it is due to the cessation of international capital movements. But in part it is due also to policy. The British tariff which has impeded imports from continental Europe has impeded the mechanism whereby the raw-material producing centres were able indirectly to liquidate their indebtedness to Great Britain. The trade agreements of Mr. Runciman, the clearing agreements of Dr. Schacht, the multitudinous clearing agreements for South-east Europe and South America have all tended in the same direction. And the persistence of currency instability, and the cessation of international capital movements which accompanies it, has prevented any mitigation of the stress which brought these policies into operation.[1] Few things are more certain than that while this state of affairs persists, international trade must stagnate, existing international investments must be in danger, and the whole movement of internal recovery which has taken place within certain of the national systems since 1933, must be regarded as liable to sudden reversal.

5. It is sometimes urged that the way out of all this chaos is to be provided by agreements, not between governments, but between local groups of producers. International agreements between national groups of producers with regard to the area of sales are to supplant the network of tariffs, quotas and licence systems in which trade is at present entangled. The attempts which have been made hitherto to liberate trade by negotiating tariff reductions have been misconceived, it is said. It is not possible to remove tariff barriers until trade conditions are stabilized. First let there be international cartels with full power to settle area

---

[1] For more detailed treatment of this part of the subject reference should be made to the annual *World Economic Survey* of the League of Nations. Mr. Folke Hilgerdt's *The Approach to Bilateralism—A Change in the Structure of World Trade* (Index, August 1935), should also be consulted.

quotas. The reduction of tariffs will then be a matter of comparative simplicity. This is not a proposal which springs from academic economists. It is a proposal which has had the support of statesmen and the heavy industries. No less a figure than M. Herriot has been at pains to write a book bearing the optimistic title, *The United States of Europe*, in which he elaborates such a project.[1] The late M. Loucheur lent it the significance of his support and his influence.

Now there can be no objection on principle to industrial arrangements that overlap national boundaries. In a world not ridden with economic nationalism, nothing would be less remarkable than that advantages of propinquity and productive convenience should lead to the formation of companies, and arrangements between companies, that were international in nature. It has often been the hope of international liberals as of international socialists that a growing internationalization of economic life would lead to a diminution of national political animosities. Given a wise international planning, the hope is still not irrational.

All this should go without saying. But it is a far cry from the recognition of the desirability of internationalized business to the belief that the international sales agreement as such is con-

---

[1] *The United States of Europe*, by Eduard Herriot; English translation by R. J. Dingle.

ducive to this end. There are indeed reasons for believing exactly the contrary.

In the first place, we must recognize that many of the existing international sales agreements are themselves dependent on the existence of tariffs and quotas. In the absence of such obstacles, they would themselves cease to operate. The authorities of the various states, convinced that it is their business to secure as large a volume as possible of sales for their local industrialists, place the apparatus of restraint of trade at the disposal of the trade associations. The quotas actually secured are the result of a process of bargaining in which the erection of restrictions, or the threat of restriction, plays a very essential part. One has only to recollect the collaboration between the British Board of Trade and the British Iron and Steel Trades Federation in the recent negotiation with the Steel Cartel to see how the mechanism works. In the absence of state assistance the British quota would have been much smaller. Speaking generally, it may be asserted that the area quota type of agreement, as it exists in continental Europe today, would be a comparatively rare phenomenon if it were not for the active support of the different states. In the absence of tariffs, it would not be to the interest of low-cost producers to make agreements with their high-cost competitors.

I

But let us ignore these practical difficulties and let us examine the proposal in the light of more general considerations. Let us suppose that, with the support of their respective governments, the high-cost and low-cost producers of the different national areas have met together and agreed upon a parcelling-out of the different markets in such a way as to obviate the necessity of any additional protection from tariffs or quotas. Is this a result conducive to a rational disposition of resources? Is this a result which achieves that division of labour between the inhabitants of the different national areas which would come about in the absence of restrictions?

Surely not. The effect of tariffs, as we have already seen, is to prevent the optimal adjustment. By raising the prices of imported goods, they make it possible for high-cost producers to remain in business. They make it possible, that is to say, for resources to be applied in lines of business which are less productive than the other lines of business which would outbid them if it were not for the existence of the tariff. They impede that international division of labour which would bring resources to the point of highest return.

But in what respect are the arrangements contemplated substantially different from this? The tariffs are to be rendered unnecessary. The high-cost production is to be protected another way.

But, so far as the disposition of resources among different lines of production is concerned, the effect is the same. The tariffs prevent the low-cost producers undercutting the others. The agreements do likewise. We may well ask, what is the benefit from the repeal of tariffs which is to follow the establishment of such a system ? To prevent the suspicion that prices are *artificially* high any longer ? The gain is a pure optical delusion. The form of restrictionism has changed. But the substance is unaltered.

The fact is, of course, that it is not the function of a rational organization of production to procure to each area its " proper share " of each and every line of industry which governments or entrepreneurs would wish to have domiciled there. The object of rational planning must be to see that the local factors of production are applied at the points of maximum productivity. And this implies that all but the industries at which the local factors are most efficient are *not* domiciled in the area. To a certain primitive outlook, highly prevalent in our own day, there is a certain intrinsic value in the presence within the local government area of different typical kinds of industry—an iron and steel industry, a textile industry, a chemical industry, a sugar-beet industry. . . . It is thought to be in some sense a national humiliation not to produce pig-iron within the borders. But the danger of war apart

—which may justify many departures from maximum productivity—if these industries do not happen to be the industries at which the local factors of production are most efficient, such an outlook is pure mysticism—and a rather infantile mysticism at that. There is no economic advantage in having iron and steel industries if iron and steel can be procured more cheaply from abroad. The logical conclusion of the attitude, which would have each area allotted its " proper share " of the different possible industries, would be complete suspension of international division of labour—national autarky by international agreement ! A tranquil condition for the " United States of Europe ".[1]

6. It is sometimes thought that all the difficulties we are discussing spring essentially from certain accidental limitations of the existing national areas. It is agreed that, given the

[1] Nevertheless if we were offered the choice between a world parcelled out into national sales areas by international cartel agreements with no tariffs, and a world split up into national markets by high protection, it is probable that we should choose the former. We have seen already that the choice is not offered. In real life, if not in the speeches of delegates to world economic conferences, the cartels depend on the tariffs. Still if we were offered the choice, the cartels would have it every time. But why ? Not because there is any important analytical difference between a market protected by duties and a market protected by agreements. But simply because, in the absence of tariffs, we could be pretty sure that the sales quota agreements would break down. Tariffs tend to stick. Monopolies tend to break. Sooner or later the low-cost producers would find the situation intolerable, and the labour of the world would come to be more rationally divided.

present multiplicity of national areas, the necessity of foreign trade must involve the most intolerable complications if internal planning of the kind we have been discussing is adopted. But it is urged that these complications could be eliminated by a suitable regrouping of national areas. If only the different areas could be regrouped into suitable economic units, it is said, the international complications would fade into insignificance.

Now there can be no doubt that, from the economic point of view, the present multiplicity of national areas is an unmitigated nuisance. So long as each sovereign state claims the right to control both the movement of goods and people, the multiplicity of states constitutes in the modern world an impediment to rational economic arrangements no less conspicuous than the mass of local restrictions and octrois in the middle ages. If some good fairy overnight could reduce the number of national boundaries by half and endow the inhabitants of the new area with sufficient common sense to co-operate sufficiently with their neighbours to maintain at least a minimum of law and order, who can doubt that it would be a most inestimable benefit ? Who can doubt the value from the economic point of view of the arrangements which have prevented the forty-eight states of the great American Federation from falling into the intolerable confusion of the states of the European mainland ? Who can doubt the value of the formation of the German Zollverein or the union of the states of South Africa ? If independent national planning could take place within areas not so grotesquely unsuited to the conduct of economic policy of any sort as the majority of national areas at the present time, then, to that extent, the logical contradictions which must accompany it would be considerably diminished.

But they would not be eliminated. Let us ignore all practical difficulties of delimiting such areas. Let us suppose that, despite the unequal endowment of different parts of the earth's surface with raw materials and facilities of production, it were found possible to carve out areas which, within limits, could achieve self-sufficiency without complete surrender of the habits and customs appropriate to modern knowledge. Nevertheless, so long as there were differences of costs of producing different commodities in the different areas so constituted, so long would there be advantage in dividing labour between them, so long would there be a loss of potential wealth if the division of labour were restricted. Either there would be no cost differences, in which case there would be no necessity for inter-regional restrictions : or there would be cost differences, in which case restriction would be a disadvantage.

Now of course it is possible to contend that, compared with the great technical advantage of planned production, sacrifices of this sort would be a matter of secondary importance. And it is quite possible to conceive of a world in which the distribution of resources was such as to render the advantages of co-operation between the different parts a comparatively negligible quantity. But in fact, given the world as it actually is, this argument is not very convincing. The distribution of resources and the distribution of people is so unequal that, however ingenious the national regroupings, it does not seem possible to arrive at arrangements which render inter-area division of labour a matter of small importance. It is not out of the question to conceive of regroupings within which self-sufficiency is possible. But it is not possible to think of regroupings within which the practice of self-sufficiency would not involve the most substantial sacrifices. The world as a whole is still poor. Can it afford such sacrifices for the aesthetic pleasures of autarkies not even based upon existing national prejudices?

The fact is, of course, that the idea of regional regrouping as it is usually propounded nowadays depends upon what is essentially a wrong conception of the purpose of international co-operation. According to this conception, the purpose of international division of labour is to enable the inhabitants of different areas to procure from abroad the materials and products which they cannot produce for themselves. And the obstacles to regional regrouping are conceived to consist essentially in the difficulty of discovering areas so self-sufficient that this necessity no longer exists. If there could be created areas, like the celebrated island of the Swiss Family Robinson, in which all the flowers and fauna of temperate, tropical and even arctic regions—to say nothing of mineral resources—existed side by side, then from this point of view everything would be perfect.

But, as we have seen already, this conception is essentially fallacious. The purpose of international division of labour is not merely to make possible the import of things which cannot be produced on the spot; it is rather to permit the resources on the spot to be devoted wholly to the production of the things they are best fitted to produce, the remainder being procured from elsewhere. The wider the market the greater the specialization possible, the greater therefore the real incomes of all parties to the exchange. The conception of international trade as the *pis aller*, as the dismal necessity, impairing the delights of an otherwise perfect self-sufficiency, is essentially the conception of an age which has not understood wherein the advantages of international trade consist. It is a sort of economic narcissism. Plausible enough as a propaganda for the interests menaced by competing imports, it can only be regarded as evidence of ignorance or of unsolved spiritual conflicts on the part of those who have nothing to lose.

It follows, therefore, that the gain from regional regrouping or wider units of any kind is not a gain of greater self-sufficiency, but a gain of the abolition of so much self-sufficiency on the part of the areas which are thus amalgamated. It is not in the fact that the tariff area of the American Federation constitutes an area which could be self-sufficient that the gain of Union consists. It is in the fact that the forty-eight states which constitute the Union are each not compelled by internal limitation of markets to a greater degree of self-sufficiency than the natural conditions of production warrant. It is not the possible self-sufficiency of the area as a whole, but the absence of self-sufficiency on the part of the constituent states, which is the advantage of the Union.

It follows, too, that any gain in productive efficiency which is secured by the abolition of " internal " obstacles is a gain which has its cost if it is secured only by the erection of obstacles around the area. From the international point of view, the tariff union is not an advantage in itself. It is an advantage only in so far as, on balance, it conduces to more extensive division of labour. It is to be justified only by arguments which would justify still more its extension to all areas capable of entering into trade relationships. The only possible vindication of the retention of old restrictions or the erection of new ones is the argument that, in their absence, the tendency to restrict would be still more rampageous. No doubt if we could coax the rest of the world into free trade by a high tariff union against the produce of the Eskimos that would be, on balance, an international gain. But it would be inferior to an arrangement whereby the Eskimos were included. The only completely innocuous tariff union would be directed against the inaccessible produce of the moon.

In practice this belief that it is possible to fight restrictionism by restriction is likely to prove a most dangerous delusion. Hope deferred maketh the heart sick. To the well-meaning internationalist anxious to stem the flood of irrationality which is threatening to overwhelm us, it is tempting to believe that by acquiescing in the idea of a little restriction he may hope to trick the interests into the abolition of much. And no doubt there are conceivable cases where the evils of high protectionism by small states are very obvious—Central Europe is perhaps a case in point—in which it should not be out of the question to secure some "concession" all round in the interests of a less irrational arrangement. But in the main it is not so. You cannot make omelettes without breaking eggs. And you cannot abolish tariff barriers anywhere without injuring some interests.[1] In the absence of a firm public

[1] It is perhaps worth noting that the most conspicuous example of a tariff union which, from the international point of view, must be

opinion persuaded of the undesirability of restrictions as such, the likelihood is either that the interests will block the whole thing, or that they will make it a pretext for the erection of new and even more iniquitous limitations. The economist can never beat the interests if he starts by playing their game. It is not that he is less intelligent. But he has less technical knowledge; and by agreeing to restrictionism at all he surrenders the issue on which he has logical superiority. To dissipate the restrictionist fallacies which at present befog public opinion may well seem to be a policy which promises less speedy results than some compromise with the opposition. But, in the long run, it is the one policy which has the ghost of a chance of success.

7. All this has the most intimate bearing on one of the most discussed of contemporary problems, the problem of the " unsatisfied " nations. It is often urged by the spokesmen of these nations that the absence of colonial possessions is a grave economic disadvantage. It deprives them of access to raw materials, of opportunities for investment and migration, of a sufficient supply of foreign exchange. And the men of goodwill

judged to have been an unqualified success, the German Zollverein, was not brought about by restrictionist measures. The duties imposed by the union were not intended to be highly protective, but rather to safeguard the revenues of the constituent states, and arrangements were made for their progressive reduction.

among the satisfied, acquiescing in the justice of these accusations, urge likewise that, in the interests of international peace and justice, it is incumbent on their governments to hand over large tracts of territory to those who were not so fortunate in the race for colonial possessions.

Now there is a problem here. Indeed, it is one of the most urgent problems of our day. But, as stated above, it rests upon misconception. It is not true that the absence of territorial possessions is a bar to the purchase of raw materials. The most important raw material of British industry during the nineteenth century—raw cotton—was purchased outside the Empire; and there is no reason whatever to suppose that anybody was a penny the worse for that. Whether cotton is purchased in Carolina or the Sudan, it has to be paid for. Provided that contracts are enforceable in both places, it is a matter of indifference whether or not they are coloured the same on the map. It is not true that it is necessary to own a country in order that investment may be made in it. The largest proportion of British external investment during the nineteenth century went to the United States of America. It is not true that an Empire is needed in order that migration may be possible. For many years more emigrants from Great Britain went to the United States than to any part of the Empire. Nor is it true that the absence of possessions abroad as such is any impediment to the possession of foreign exchange. A debt to Canada is the same as a debt to the Argentine; the one is no more difficult to liquidate than the other. All these arguments, the stock counters of contemporary discussion, involve crude fallacy. They do not touch the root of the matter at all.

For the root of the matter is not possession but exclusion. If the Colonial Empires are reserved areas for trade and investment and migration, then the inhabitants of the areas which have not similar reserved areas have a very substantial grievance. If they are not permitted to sell their goods to these areas save on inferior terms, they do not so readily acquire the power to purchase their raw materials; they cannot divide labour so extensively. If they are not permitted to invest there, their capital has to be invested at an inferior margin. If they are debarred from immigration, they have to suffer the ills of relative over-population. These are real grievances which, if realized, may provoke men to the shedding of blood. If they were not wrapped up in the fallacies of the policies of autarky and power, they would carry overwhelming conviction to all disinterested minds. When Dr. Schacht says that, because his country does not own more territory, he is short of foreign exchange, he is using the language of fallacy. But if he says that discrimination against German goods, in territories which are not possessed by Germany, tends to turn the terms of trade against Germany and so makes the foreign exchange position and the purchase of raw materials more difficult, he is stating a fact which no candid person can deny.

It is obvious that such considerations have the most profound significance for the future policy of the British Empire. So long as Great Britain adhered to the policy of the " open door ", it was no empty claim that those parts of the Empire which were administered from at home were administered as if in trust for the world as a whole —we had no responsibility for the protectionism of the Dominions. So long as foreign goods were admitted free and foreign investment and foreign settlement not discriminated against, the Englishman was not economically better off than the foreigner because his country had wide possessions.[1] The myopic apostles of continental reaction who never understood the principles of classical liberalism, their minds befuddled with the leaden clangour of another imperial idea, may have denied this. But their accusations do not hold water. The administration of the free-trade Empire is not one of those episodes of history of which Englishmen need be ashamed. No foreigner was poorer because of the width of our territories,

---

[1] The advantages of government employment to the middle classes were probably never financially greater than the expenses of defence and administration.

so long as these principles were adhered to. If he said he was, he can only have been hoping that if his government possessed them it would administer them on different principles.

But with the passing of free trade and with the coming of the Ottawa system all this has changed. We have joined with the protectionist parts of the Empire to exclude the products of the foreigner. We have imposed limitations on the import into the poorer parts of the Empire of cheap goods from Japan. We can no longer claim that the peoples of the nations without colonies are no worse off because of our policy. It is just these peoples who have been hit. We have erected a fence round the Empire. The factors of production elsewhere must now work at inferior margins. In this we are no worse than the other protectionist Powers. It is not to be believed that if the Empire as a whole were handed over to Germany or Japan it would be administered on free-trade lines; it is indeed the victory in Great Britain of the retrograde German ideology of exploitation and power which has been responsible for the ruin of the splendid principles of internationalism and freedom.[1] We are not worse than the unsatisfied. But perhaps we are more vulnerable.

[1] It would be very easy to show the direct German inspiration of the English Tariff Reform movement. The ideas of Ashley, Cunningham and many others were of obvious German origin. The spiritual home of modern British Imperialism is the shelf which holds the verbose proceedings of the *Verein für Sozialpolitik*. The

It is the tragedy of such a situation that, short of a complete reversal of policy, there is no way out. There is no ultimate solution by a mere redistribution of territory. If we were to make the most stupendous effort of altruism and were to hand over to the unsatisfied Powers large blocks of the Empire, the problem would still exist. If there were to be a war and we were to be defeated and shorn of all our possessions, the grievance would merely have shifted its habitation. There is no conceivable repartition of the earth's surface which would be permanently satisfactory.

What is needed is not repartition but the lowering of all those barriers to trade and investment and migration which afford a real pretext for the argument that the accident of history which gave the governments of some areas less of the territories of this world was also an accident which doomed the inhabitants of these areas to a position of avoidable economic inferiority. Until that is done, the danger of war will persist.

<small>changes in British Fiscal Policy of 1932, which were among the last embarrassments of German Political Democracy, sprang from the influence of those German scholars whose lives were devoted to undoing the work of the *Aufklärungszeit*. Interesting case-material for M. Benda!</small>

CHAPTER VI

INTERNATIONAL PLANNING OF PARTICULAR LINES OF INDUSTRY

1. IN the last chapter we have been considering interstate planning of particular channels of trade. We have examined the significance of bilateralism and international sales quotas and the implications of proposals for regional regrouping. We have glanced at the bearing of all this on recent discussions of the colonial problem. We must now consider another type of policy—the international planning of particular lines of industry. Admitted that the attempt to plan trade by geographical units, or arrangements between geographical units, is likely to lead to difficulty, may we not hope for a solution by planning, not on geographical, but on industrial lines ? May we not achieve international economy by organizing each industry on an international basis ?

It is to the discussion of this question that the present chapter is devoted. It should be borne in mind throughout that we shall be discussing only the planning of particular lines of production in isolation. The planning of international production as a whole is a problem we shall discuss later.

2. International control of particular lines of production is a comparatively recent development of industrial organization. In certain branches of manufacturing industry, international sales quota arrangements of the type we discussed in the last chapter were beginning to make their appearance even before the war. In certain lines of production the organization of production into national groups had made considerable progress, especially in areas of high protection. But, speaking broadly, before the war the formation of international organizations attempting to regulate international production was a very exceptional occurrence. Agreements between governments giving statutory sanction to such arrangements were almost completely unheard of. " Twenty-five years ago ", says Mr. Rowe, " anyone who prophesied that the world supply of most of the important primary products would be subject to artificial control, as a result of agreements between the producers or their governments, would not have commanded one minute's attention from economists or business men." [1]

The war, however, greatly altered the relation of governments to the organization of production.

[1] *Markets and Men*, p. 2.

The exigencies of war necessitated (or were thought to necessitate) governmental control of production ; and the obvious administrative convenience of being able to negotiate concerning such controls with representatives of the different groups of national producers led governments, not merely to encourage, but often to enforce, the formation of associations for this purpose. All over the world, producers, who hitherto had lived in fear and trembling of accusations of monopolistic combination, suddenly found themselves urged to combine to form groups which could speak for " the industry " as a whole. This happened not merely in manufacturing industry, where other tendencies towards greater centralization were sometimes already in operation, but in agricultural and extractive industries where no tendency to combination existed, or was even likely to exist, in the absence of governmental encouragement.

When the war ceased these organizations persisted. And when, as a result of the vast changes in the conditions of supply and demand which the change over from war conditions necessitated, some groups of producers found themselves in difficulties, they tended to resort to collective action to attempt to remedy the position. They formed pools and restriction schemes. They invoked the assistance of their governments; and not infrequently this assistance was forthcoming.

The period between the armistice and the coming of the Great Depression is marked by the spread of national restriction schemes—the trade unions of the agricultural and raw material producers.

These schemes were not very fortunate. For the time being indeed they succeeded in maintaining prices. But they did not succeed in controlling production. Even when production was nationally controlled, international competition was stimulated. The over-investments of the boom period were, in part at least, the result of the stimulus of high prices brought about by restriction. Vast stocks accumulated in the commodity markets, a growing menace to stability. And when the boom broke, they collapsed. We do not read the lesson of the depression correctly if we do not recognize the extent to which its severity was enhanced by the collapse of restriction schemes.

It might have been thought that the effect of all this would have been to suggest suspicion of the general desirability of such agreements. In the pre-war industrial structure the collapse of a boom did not work such widespread havoc. The secular fluctuations of demand for particular products were met by a gradual adjustment of the competitive mechanism. The less efficient units closed down. The capital and labour were transferred elsewhere. Hard as this might be in individual cases, there can be little doubt that it

CH. VI INDUSTRIAL PLANNING 133

was conducive to changes which were favourable to the vast body of consumers. There was more stability in a system which yielded at once to change than in a system which did not yield till it snapped.

But this was not the moral drawn by the governments and the producers. They urged that there had been, not too much, but too little restriction, that what was wanted was the erection of controls which should be so all-embracing as to preclude the rise of outside competitors. Accordingly, like the poet who was worsted only to fight better, they proceeded to organize restriction on an even vaster scale.

For this purpose the producers in the different national areas were induced to enter international agreements, allotting to each group a proportionate share of an aggregate production fixed by the periodic deliberations of a central control. If the producers showed any reluctance, the governments themselves intervened. At the present time a substantial proportion of the so-called primary production of the world is subject to national or international controls of this sort. And, not merely by the groups of producers interested, but also by many who profess to take a wider view of the criteria of successful industrial organization, they are coming to be regarded as essential features of the " ordered society of the future ". As in the middle ages under the guild system, the different local economies were organized into groups of local producers, differentiated according to their products, so, in the twentieth century, the world economy is to be organized into groups of international producers, differentiated on a similar basis. International planning is to proceed on industrial lines.

3. But it is just here that difficulty arises. Here, as in the case of the restrictions on trade which we have discussed already, it is easy enough to understand the developments which have taken place as the make-shift expedients of desperate situations. But it is not easy to understand the state of mind of persons, other than the producers who benefit, who regard them as something which it would be desirable to make permanent.

We may concede immediately that, if restrictionism of this sort is to be practised, arrangements which control the production of all producers are greatly to be preferred to arrangements which control the production of only a part. If the price of any commodity is to be maintained at a point above the competitive level, it is necessary to control the total supply. If this is not done, the experiment is doomed to disaster. Outside competition grows, over-production is encouraged, and sooner or later the market collapses in an atmosphere of panic bankruptcy. Mr. Walter

CH. VI   INDUSTRIAL PLANNING   135

Elliot and others who have attempted price maintenance without control of supply may question this. But the verdict of history will be against them. If restrictionism of this sort is to be practised at all, then the new restrictionism is superior to the old.

But this raises the fundamental question —Is this kind of restrictionism really desirable ? It is clear that it is a form of planning. It is clear that it is a form of planning which may bring financial advantage to those participating in it. But is it a form of planning which can be regarded as being in the social interest ? Are its effects likely to be such as to be capable of being regarded as part of an international plan calculated to benefit, not merely the participating producers, but the citizens of the world as a whole ? The wiseacres of administration, who tend to regard any organization which works as a good thing in itself, may be greatly impressed by these vast and ambitious schemes. But before we can share their complacency we must be convinced, not merely that the organization works, but also that it works for purposes which the citizens of the world would approve.

Now, so far as the sale of goods actually produced is concerned, it may be admitted that restriction by production quotas has much to commend it above the restriction of area of sales, discussed in the last chapter. Once the volume to be sold has been determined by the control, the amount released for sale is sold in the world market at prices which do not discriminate between different geographical groups of consumers. Unless governments choose to complicate matters by tariffs and quotas, we do not witness the phenomenon of differences of prices unjustified by differences in costs of transport, etc. On the assumption that, in the market, one man is to be regarded as being as good as another, and that therefore it is not fair that different prices should have to be paid by different people for similar units of a given world supply, this is obviously superior to a regime of divided markets.

But as regards the distribution of resources between different lines of production and the determination of the volume of production in general, both forms of restriction are open to the same fundamental objection. They both tend to stereotype the conditions of production in favour of the high-cost producers. They tend, that is to say, to make the production of the high-cost producers greater, and the production of the low-cost producers less, than would be dictated by the requirements of a rational allocation of resources. Moreover, they tend to make production as a whole less than it otherwise would be. The dilemma is unescapable. Either the quotas are the same as they would be without restriction—in which case they are unnecessary—or they are different—in which case they are harmful. There is no third alternative.

This drawback would probably be generally admitted. That restrictionism restricts is not a proposition which would be often contested. Nor is it really open to question that it restricts in the interests of those producers whose costs are highest—that is to say, those producers whose resources would first be transferred to other lines of production in a rational organization of production. But it is often said that, while it may have this " static " disadvantage, it has the compensating " dynamic " advantages that it evens out fluctuations through time. It keeps things steady. It facilitates more orderly adaptation.

But this is to misconceive the nature of the argument just developed. To demonstrate that the production quota arrangement favours high-cost production is not merely to demonstrate that it involves the " static " disadvantage that production is less and takes place at higher average cost than need otherwise have been the case ; it is to demonstrate also that the adaptation of the productive apparatus is impeded by the selfsame arrangements. To keep high-cost producers alive is to prevent " dynamic " adjustment. The restriction scheme means, not only that *at any moment* the volume of production is restricted ; it means also that *from moment to moment* the more efficient producers are prevented from displacing the less. If this is not a dynamic disadvantage it would be interesting to know what is.[1]

It is sometimes said that such restrictions are desirable because, if prices are not maintained now, then, later on, supplies will be endangered. If voluntary restriction is not practised now, then involuntary restriction, arising from a shortage of productive equipment, will occur in the future. What appears to be merely in the interest of the producers is in fact in the interest of the consumers also. Sentiments of this sort are not restricted to the Howiesons and the Hatrys.

It is not easy, however, to find cases where such a shortage has actually happened. There is no conspicuous case where scarcity has been brought about by the absence of restriction. Indeed, it is not very easy to see the causation of such a process. Presumably if prices are allowed to fall, some producers go out of business. But this does not mean that their plant necessarily goes out of operation. It can be taken over by enterprise not encumbered by the old capitalization. It will only go out of operation if the cost of working

[1] The operation of the Tin Restriction Scheme is a good example. According to Mr. Rowe, if the consumer of tin could get stability of price he might not mind paying a little more than the competitive price. " But when the well-known chairman of one of the biggest tin mining companies in Malaya assures him that the East could produce at a profit all the tin required by the World at £100 per ton, and he is paying £230, the manufacturers and others naturally consider that the price of stability is altogether too high and that the tin restriction scheme is nothing more nor less than a grasping monopoly."—*Markets and Men*, pp. 166-167.

it is greater than the prevailing price. And if that is so, then it is rational that it should be abandoned. For the cost of working it is determined by the prospective prices which the necessary resources could get for other kinds of production. But if they can get better prices elsewhere than in this particular line of business it is rational that they should go there.

We may be assured, then, that, under competition, plant will not be allowed to go derelict unless it has definitely a negative value—which would certainly not be the case if the prospective demand for its products were such as to justify talk of a prospective scarcity. It is urged, however, that the scarcity may arise nevertheless, because, if the value of existing capital is not preserved, a sufficient supply of new capital will not be forthcoming. New investors will not appear, because old investments have lost their value.

This argument is not intrinsically illogical; it is quite conceivable that investors might react in this way. But there seems no reason to suppose that in fact they do so. Hitherto in the history of the world the shrinkage of the value of old investment on account of the lack of foresight of investors in the past does not seem to have had a deterrent effect on the conduct of new investors. There is no evidence that willingness to put money into what is believed to be a good thing has been diminished by the fact that in the past some people have lost their money. The conspicuous cases of shyness of this sort have arisen, not when the losses have been the result of private miscalculation, but when they have been the result of arbitrary acts of confiscation or default by governments. Indeed, if this shyness were at all general it would be hard to see why the organizers of restriction schemes are so anxious to obtain governmental sanction to prevent new investment within their own industry. If investors were not willing to risk capital in developments in which they think they see a profit, the need to limit the operation of low-cost producers would surely appear less urgent.

In fact, when we look at the broad effects of restrictionism on the scale on which it is at present practised, not in one but in many branches of industry, the boot seems to be very much on the other leg. So far from restrictionism being conducive to a free flow of new investment—new openings for capital being restricted in order that new capital may be forthcoming—it is arguable that in fact it works strongly in the other direction. The various restrictions which are imposed have the effect of lowering the rate of return on new investment. When the field of investment is restricted the rate tends to fall. The investor who might have put money into developing the business of a low-cost producer has to look elsewhere for an opening. In the long run, no doubt,

INDUSTRIAL PLANNING

some opening is forthcoming. But if, as seems probable, the rate of return is lower than he expects, he is likely to hesitate before committing himself. He says, " Things can't be as bad as all this. I'll wait and see if something better doesn't turn up "—and keeps his money on deposit at the bank. This of course tends to lower the velocity of circulation : that is to say, it is definitely deflationary.

Thus, in the last analysis, restrictionism, which is defended on the mistaken ground that the rise of prices which it promotes is good for trade, is instrumental in preventing that rise of prices which, coming from spontaneously renewed investment, might be regarded as beneficial. It is not an accident that the crisis in which resort has been made most extensively to this expedient has also been the crisis in which recovery has been slowest in making its appearance. In the short run restrictionism is deflationary. In the long run, as we have seen, it is conducive to general productive inefficiency. If producers in one line of industry practise restrictionism, it is conceivable that they may make gains which compensate them for the obvious risks they run. But if others follow suit—then these gains may well be offset by a slowing-up of the general rate of progress.

4. The disadvantages of international industrial planning are not limited to the field of pro-

duction and distribution. Almost equally with the disadvantages of geographical planning, they extend to the field of politics. They involve corruption. They involve inter-governmental friction. They involve a political structure which is dangerous to democracy.

They do this in various ways. In the first place, since the allocation of quotas almost inevitably necessitates the intervention of governments, there exists an incentive to the political organization of local bodies of producers. As with tariffs, so with restriction; if the local producers do not themselves organize so as to be in a position " to speak with one voice to the government ", the government takes steps to call such organizations into being. How well we know the trade associations, with their secretaries and their presidents and their *soi-disant* experts, hanging around the lobbies of the legislature and waiting in the ante-rooms of Ministers, trying to get a bit more " for the industry ". It is no exaggeration to say that, at the present day, these bodies, together with the trade unions—with whom they are often in a somewhat precarious alliance—are one of the dominating influences in politics all over the world. This influence is not healthy. It is an influence which brings it about that important issues are decided not on merit but by the pull of vested interests. It is an influence which places political independence and dispassionate

CH. VI   INDUSTRIAL PLANNING   143

consideration of the common weal more and more at a disadvantage.

"The member of parliament who supports every proposal for strengthening . . . monopoly is sure to acquire not only the reputation of understanding trade, but great popularity and influence with an order of men whose numbers and wealth render them of great importance. If he opposes them on the contrary, and still more if he has authority enough to be able to thwart them, neither the most acknowledged probity, nor the highest rank, nor the greatest public services, can protect him from the most infamous abuse and detraction, from personal insults, nor, sometimes, from real danger arising from the insolent outrage of furious and disappointed monopolists." [1] These words were written some time ago. But the march of time has not invalidated the diagnosis.

The damage is not confined to internal politics. The negotiations between the governments regarding the allocation of quotas are themselves productive of friction and inefficiency. The governments which represent the high-cost producers want one policy. The governments which represent the low-cost producers want another. If there is not to be a complete breakdown, there must be some *quid pro quo* elsewhere. Decisions on fundamentally separate issues are made interdependent as part of a bargaining strategy. The

[1] *Wealth of Nations* (Cannan's Edition), vol. i. p. 436.

settlement of disputes between the different parts of an industry becomes an important feature of international diplomacy.

But this is not all. The states which represent the different groups of producers taken together have an interest which is opposed to the interest of the states which represent only groups of consumers. The restrictive policy of the states of the producers may become a grave source of irritation in their relations with the states of the consumers. The apprehension which was caused in the United States of America by the policy of the British Rubber Restriction is well known. It does not seem likely that the fact that rubber restriction has now become internationalized will do very much to allay it. Nor does it seem that the policy, which is sometimes suggested, of placing a " representative of the consumers " on the governing bodies of the restriction schemes is any real cure for the difficulty. Possibly small difficulties might be smoothed over in this way. But it cannot solve the great difficulty that the interests of consumers are almost necessarily opposed to the interests of particular groups of producers when these producers act as a unity. It is a difficulty which no amount of polite mechanism is eventually capable of concealing.

5. But this brings us to the central and fundamental difficulty of this whole trend of policy—

the contradiction necessarily involved in any attempt to plan particular lines of industry in isolation.

Let us suppose that all the incidental difficulties that we have discovered so far are resolved. Let us suppose, if it is desired, that the control of a particular line of industry is truly internationalized; that the different governments take no direct hand in its management; that the divers interests of the groups of producers are financially amalgamated, so that, if it is thought expedient, high-cost units can be bought out and closed down; that there is no pressure to maintain special branches in special areas. Let us suppose even that the ——— industry is socialized as part of a world state; that the world state has undertaken " to put the affairs of the ——— industry in order ", the producers being " incapable of doing it for themselves ".

Even so, it is submitted, the whole principle of organization rests upon a total misconception of the object to which any policy which seeks the good of society as a whole, rather than the good of a limited part, should be directed. The object of such a policy, whether on liberal or socialist lines, must be to maintain the application of the different resources of society at the point at which they are most productive. Now such an object cannot be conceived in terms of the prosperity of particular industries. At every moment, it is true, the

L

actual distribution of factors can be exhibited, for statistical purposes, as a series of groups labelled " industries ". But it is of the essence of the conception of an optimal adjustment to changing needs that the contents and size of these groups should be continually shifting. Indeed, there is no reason to suppose that the classification itself will remain appropriate for any length of time. For the technical processes which give sanction to the classification are not processes which have value as such. They have value only in relation to demand : and if demand changes, the economic status of the technical processes changes also. The economic optimum is not to be attained by maintaining an " iron industry ", a " cotton industry ", a " boot and shoe industry ", a " transport industry " and so on. It is to be attained by using the factors of production in those processes in which they are most productive of the essentially changing pattern of commodities which the citizens of the world demand. As conditions change, its attainment must necessarily involve the expansion or initiation of some " industries ", the contraction and even elimination of others. If the statistical classification "*the* ——— industry" is given, as it were, an economic status, if institutions are created which bring it about that " it " acts as a unity, if the maintenance of " its " prosperity is the be-all and end-all of policy, then not only is the end of rational policy misconceived, it is likely also to be frustrated. If the controllers of each factor of production acting separately—acting " atomistically ", as is sometimes said by those who advocate "more organic" conceptions—strive continually for the highest return, there is harmony between its interest and the interests of society. " Atomistic " units do not gain by restriction of their own output. But if groups of factors with powers of exclusion and restriction do likewise, there is no necessary harmony at all. The interest of the industrial group as such is often in flagrant contradiction with the interests of society. The group may gain by restriction ; society only by plenty. It does not matter much whether the group is a group of capitalists or peasant proprietors, professional men or trade unionists. If they are given the power of exclusion, on occasion they tend to use it. Nor are things greatly changed if "*the* ——— industry" is a state or an interstate body. So long as it acts as a unit and policy is directed to *its* maintenance and improvement, so long is there danger that the ends of rational planning may be frustrated. " *The* " industry, equally with " *the* " nation, is an inappropriate instrument for the rational organization of resources.

These fears are not purely speculative. They are realized whenever and wherever such institutions come into being. They are abundantly exemplified in the effects of the industrial organization of medieval Europe, the guild system, which was essentially a system of monopolies of producers operating under governmental supervision.[1] And in our own day, with the decline of competition and the revival of similar institutions, the same contradictions come to light.

Let us take, for example, the case of agriculture. It would probably be generally agreed that in a world of advancing agricultural technique the optimal distribution of resources would show an ever-diminishing proportion directed to the production of the cruder kinds of food. If an isolated producer were to discover more efficient methods of getting wheat or potatoes, he would not continue to devote the same proportion of time to this line of production. He would devote less to this, more to the satisfaction of wants which were more elastic. Similarly with society. If the application of scientific methods to agri-

---

[1] " Though the crafts differed considerably from place to place in the amount of internal authority and political influence they enjoyed, their economic organization was alike throughout Europe. Everywhere its fundamental traits were the same. It was here that the spirit of protectionism inherent in medieval urban economy showed itself most vigorously. . . . The counterpart of the privilege enjoyed by the guild was the destruction of all initiative. No one was permitted to harm others by methods which enabled him to produce more cheaply and more quickly than they. Technical progress took on the appearance of disloyalty. The ideal was stable conditions in a stable industry." This passage is not by Adam Smith or by some similar " superficial " and " unhistorical " classical economist. It is by no less a person than Professor Henri Pirenne, one of the most justly celebrated and admired of contemporary medieval historians. Pirenne, *The Economic and Social History of Medieval Europe*, pp. 185-186.

cultural production permits us to grow the same unit of wheat with a greatly diminished application of effort, a rational planning of production would bring it about that that branch of agriculture declined, either absolutely if the population was stationary, or at least proportionately to the whole, if the population was growing. We should not proceed to take steps to preserve "*the*" wheat-producing industry at the same size, just because we had read in books that in olden days wheat production was " much the most important industry ". Yet at the present day this is just what is being done. And it is being done not merely by spontaneous restriction by independent groups of producers. It is being done also by departments of state charged with the fortunes of "*the*" agricultural industry. Everywhere Ministers of Agriculture are busily engaged in frustrating the progress of scientific invention, in attempting to preserve the occupational distribution of the censuses of thirty years ago. " It would be a shocking thing if the numbers of wheat producers were to diminish ", they say.[1] But if the end of production is the satisfaction of wants,

---

[1] Mr. Walter Elliot sometimes evades this limit of absurdity by beating the big drum about the scientific progress which renders it unnecessary to import from abroad—" abroad " being, in the interests of Canada, Australia, etc., conveniently left undefined. As we have seen above (Chap. III, paras. 2 and 3) this is no less a fallacy. But one trembles to think to what rhetorical stratagems this energetic man would have resort to defend his no doubt multitudinous activities, if he were Minister of Agriculture in a world state !

rather than the satisfaction of a sort of kindergarten aesthetic of the lay-out of the productive apparatus, it would not be shocking at all. It is exactly in harmony with the probable requirements of a scientifically progressive society.

The case of agriculture cannot be said to be inconspicuous. But it may be urged that it is not representative. All sorts of " social " and military considerations dictate the policies of governments in regard to agricultural production. It may be urged that it is not to be regarded as typical of the way policy usually develops when attention is paid to the organization of industries as units rather than to the distribution of resources between industries.

Let us therefore take another example, which at the present day is hardly less conspicuous. In some countries railways are owned by private interests. In some countries they are owned by the state. But in all countries, policy as regards the railways has this common characteristic, that their prosperity must be maintained, that their proportionate importance as means of transport must not be allowed to diminish. Whether as a result of pressure from railway shareholders and trade unionists, or whether on the spontaneous initiative of the Minister responsible for railways, policy is directed to impeding such competition from new forms of transport as might impair the value of capital already invested in the industry.

It may be in the guise of redressing a balance of taxation between different forms of transport.[1] It may be by way of absolute restriction of new entrants to the field of road transport: the principle is the same. The value of capital, governmental and otherwise, already invested in the industry must not be impaired.

But this is the very negation of progress. For progress necessarily involves the destruction of existing capital values. Imagine what would have been the condition of " the industry of rail transport " itself if preservation of the value of capital invested in stage coaches and turnpike trusts had been made the criterion of policy. It was surely quite as " sad " to witness the disappearance of that glamorous apparatus as it is to witness the scrapping of a few tank engines and the closing-down of a few branch lines. But in those days industries were not organized as units; and the fact that effort was more productive in rail transport than on the roads was regarded—and rightly regarded—as a sufficient justification for the change. If it had been regarded as a principle of policy at all costs to maintain a " coaching industry " of a certain size and a certain capital value, can there be any doubt that the resources

[1] If railways are in fact overtaxed, there can naturally be no objection to readjustments of the tax system, provided it stops at redressing the real injustice. But this is no justification for many of the forms of taxation of road vehicles that have actually been introduced.

of society would have been wrongly distributed ?[1]

They would not only have been wrongly distributed ; they would also have been distributed in such a way as to create positions of privilege for some and positions of disadvantage for others. And if the process of organizing industries as units becomes widespread, be it on a national or international scale, the creation of such privileged sections must necessarily become more and more conspicuous. If groups of producers are allowed to organize themselves and to restrict new entrants and new investment " in order to maintain the stability of the industry ", the capital and labour which is excluded has to work elsewhere for prospects which presumably it finds less attractive. Thus gradually, on the one hand, there is built up a series of entrenched industrial interests, labour being combined with capital in the fight against interlopers, and on the other hand there develop residues of, as it were, pariah labour and pariah capital, either working at margins less productive than the margins of "organized industry", or unemployed through unwillingness to accept the lower remuneration necessarily associated with the inferior margins. This is not an imaginary

---

[1] It is amusing to note that the claim that is sometimes made for the motor car that " it revives the business of the roads " rests essentially on the same mercantilistic basis as the claim that it would be disastrous if the business of the railways were to diminish. The special pleading of particular lines of industry is almost always protectionist in spirit.

picture. It is a picture of what does happen and what must happen whenever, by the erection of industrial castes, capital and labour are prevented from serving society in those lines of production in which they are willing to offer their services. It happened in the middle ages. It is happening today. And there is no way out save the supersession of this method of planning by methods based on completely different principles.

For, as should be abundantly plain by now, the principle of organizing industries as units and making their prosperity the criterion of social welfare, although often put forward as an alternative to the chaos of protectionism and nationalism, is in fact only another manifestation of the same underlying tendency. The protectionist who wishes to save " *the* ——— industry " by preventing the competition of foreign products, and the planner who wishes to save it by excluding the incursion of interloping capital and labour, are misled by the same fundamental fallacy—the "*the* industry" fallacy we may call it. In the last analysis it is a manifestation of the apparently chronic tendency of the human mind to regard cost as the creator of value ; to argue that, because labour has been expended on a product, therefore it ought to be regarded as valuable ; and that if it is not so regarded, then steps should be taken to bring it about that it is. It is a manifestation of the tendency to regard the instruments of production as such as valuable without regard for the demand for their products, that tendency which regards it as being the duty of statecraft to adapt demand to the maintenance of the value of the instruments of production, rather than to make the value of instruments of production depend upon their satisfaction of a free demand. No doubt these tendencies spring from habits of thought more congenial to the unsophisticated intelligence than the habit of regarding value as being of subjective origin, and the utility of the instruments of production as derived from their capacity to serve consumption. It is easier to appraise the industry that has been preserved than the consumption which has been sacrificed, the balance-sheets that have been saved than the products which might have been created. Nevertheless, if the human race is ever to manage its affairs on a rational basis it must transcend these primitive habits. It must learn to think less of industries as ends in themselves, more of the ends to which they may be instrumental. It must think less of the organization of particular industries, more of the organization of the whole complex of productive activity.

6. It is sometimes said that the unification of industries is inevitable : that the amalgamation of all productive units engaged in turning out particular kinds of commodities is implicit in the

main tendencies of the evolution of industry : and that whether we like it or not, if we wish to avoid the difficulties and contradictions implicit in this form of organization, we must at least accept it as a starting-point and build our plans upon it.

Now, it may be true that these developments are inevitable in the sense that they will actually come about. It may be that the present tendencies in this direction are so strong that nothing that can be said against them, however reasonable, can suffice to arrest them. It is clear that they grow day by day and that the most powerful political parties, both of the right and of the left, are almost equally involved in supporting them.

But do not let us deceive ourselves. If it does happen, it will happen because men have willed it should happen, not because of any inherent necessities in the technique of industry or the spontaneous play of free enterprise. It is not true that the technique of any important industry is such as to make desirable in any sense the concentration of world production in one technical production unit. Even in the industries demanding the heaviest mechanical equipment, the optimal size of the technical production unit is usually much below that size which could supply the population of a small country, let alone the population of the entire planet. And in most industries, especially in primary production, the optimal production units are of much smaller dimensions.

Nor is it true that that tendency to amalgamation among producers, which arises not for reasons of technical convenience but in order to influence the market, is generally such as to bring about hard and fast organizations of the kind we have been discussing. Where such organizations exist they are usually in one way or another the creation of policy. So far as primary production is concerned it is notorious that the various restriction schemes tend to break up if they do not receive statutory authorization. And although, in manufacturing industry, spontaneous combination has more independent vitality, it is hard to find cases of long-lasting international monopoly which are not based on the grants of special patent rights or on the existence of other statutory restrictions of outside competition, tariffs, quotas and the like. The contrast between the relative freedom of Great Britain from the grosser forms of industrial monopoly during the free-trade era and the rapid growth of such phenomena since the erection of tariffs is highly significant in this connection. So again is the contrast between pre-war Great Britain under free trade and Germany under protection.[1] This is not to deny that there does exist a genuine problem of a monopoly in the

[1] On the connection between protection and monopoly in Germany see Röpke, *German Commercial Policy*, especially pp. 30-39.

INDUSTRIAL PLANNING

case of certain types of public utility undertakings or undertakings enjoying local protection by high costs of transport. Nor is it to deny that the existing structure of the law under so-called free capitalism leaves much to be desired as a framework for genuinely free enterprise. But, speaking broadly, it can be said without fear of effective contradiction that, in a world free from trade restrictions and statutory support for monopoly, the tendency of free enterprise to break down monopolistic positions would be sufficiently strong in all save the most exceptional cases to make any talk of a general and spontaneous tendency to unification of all industries completely out of touch with reality.

The tendency for industries to be organized as single units, either nationally or internationally, exists. But it exists in the main because men acting as political citizens have willed that it should exist. It is no inherent tendency of a system of free enterprise. If we suffer from its consequences, we suffer not from necessity but from choice.

CHAPTER VII

INTERNATIONAL REGULATION OF WAGES AND HOURS OF LABOUR

1. IN the last chapter we surveyed the implications of the international planning of particular lines of production. We found such plans to be defective in that, in one form or another, they all take as their criterion the prosperity of particular groups of the factors of production, rather than the proper apportionment of all factors between all groupings in which they might possibly be employed. We found that, in making the industry the unit of organization, they actually constituted a nucleus of resistance to change, not different in kind from the resistances constituted by nationalistic organization. We found, that is to say, that they simply tended to preserve in a new form the irrationality of existing arrangements.

In this chapter we have to examine the problem in yet another aspect. It is sometimes said that the international chaos, which is the product of unco-ordinated national planning, is to be

CH. VII   WAGES AND HOURS OF LABOUR   159

attributed to differences in conditions of labour. The multiplication of tariffs and quotas, the chronic fear of underselling by the foreigner, the probable reluctance of states to allow the products of nationalized industry to be displaced by the competition of cheaper imports from abroad, are all explained as arising from the existence of differences in wages and hours of labour in the different national areas. If only these differences could be levelled out by international regulation, it is said, the consequential difficulties would disappear. This is clearly a claim which deserves the most careful investigation. Accordingly it is to such an investigation that the present chapter is devoted. Incidentally we shall find that the conclusions to which we shall be led will throw some light on some of the propositions already employed in the analysis of earlier chapters. We shall find, too, that they are a useful preliminary to the analysis of some of the proposals for complete international planning which we have to discuss later on.

2. Let us commence by investigating the effects of international equalization of wage rates. It is of course most improbable that such an equalization would actually be attempted : the political obstacles are much too formidable. But it is the inequality of wage rates which, according to the views we have to discuss, is responsible for much

of the present national restrictionism : and our object here is not so much to judge the practicability of the policy of removing such inequality, but rather to judge of its effects, if it were practicable.

Since we are discussing a hypothetical case, we are justified in considerable simplification. Let us therefore abstract from all political difficulties of authorizing and supervising such regulation. In the world we are now to discuss there will be no evasion, no repudiation of international conventions. What is decreed is executed. Let us assume that the world is divided into two national areas only. Let us assume that throughout these areas there exists a regime of competitive industry and that money based upon gold is in general use. Let us assume further that within each area the labourers are all of one fundamental grade of skill, although special labourers may in course of time have become specialized to particular industries : we may assume, therefore, that *within* each area there exists some tendency to a common rate of wages. But let us assume also, for reasons we will not yet investigate, that, *between* the areas, rates of wages measured in gold are very unequal. To lend some concreteness to the discussion let us call the high-wage area " America " and the low-wage area " Japan ". But in order not to confuse these hypothetical areas with the real ones,

CH. VII   WAGES AND HOURS OF LABOUR   161

let us continually use inverted commas.

Our apparatus is now ready. Let us commence to use it by discussing a most improbable example. Let us suppose—what is not improbable—that in our hypothetical " America ", where wage rates are high, when trade is opened, there is apprehension of competition from " Japan ", where rates are low. The " American " industrialists, indignant that certain of their industries are in danger of being undercut by the products of " cheap labour ", refer the matter to an international tribunal. Let us then suppose—what is very improbable—that the tribunal decides to equalize the " unfair " labour conditions *by reducing " American " wages to the " Japanese " level.* (The friends of the International Labour Office at Geneva will observe that we are here contemplating a type of policy not likely to be recommended by that organization.)

What are the implications of this policy ? The conspicuous feature, surely, is that " American " labour costs are greatly reduced. (Whether they are reduced in strict proportion to the wage-cut, or whether they are reduced rather less than proportionately owing to injurious repercussions on physique and morale, is a matter we need not discuss : we may assume that the cut in rates is such as to more than outweigh all adverse reactions on productivity.) That is to say that costs of production in general are reduced and,

M

with costs, the prices at which "American" products can be marketed at a profit. Imagine, for example, the price at which Ford cars could be sold if, in the real America, wage rates were cut to actual Japanese levels. The "Japanese" menace is at an end. Indeed the boot is now on the other leg. "Japanese" products are likely to be undersold very generally, both in "Japan" and in "America". Imports into "America" fall. Exports from "America" rise. In "Japan" the reverse process is to be witnessed. There occurs a drain of gold from "Japan" to "America". If this is not speedily allowed to affect the wage level in each country by restoring some degree of inequality, there will be unemployment and idle capacity in "Japan" and some sort of inflationary boom in "America".

Let us now assume a less improbable experiment. Let us assume that the international tribunal to which appeal has been made adopts a more humanitarian policy. Let us assume that it decides, not to grind "American" wage rates down to the "Japanese" level, but to raise the "Japanese" level to the "American".

What happens? Surely something that is essentially similar to what happened before. The relationship between costs has been changed *in the same direction*. It is, of course, just conceivable, if the "American" demand were sufficiently inelastic and the wage differences

CH. VII WAGES AND HOURS OF LABOUR 163

sufficiently small, that "Japanese" receipts might be maintained—or even rise. It is conceivable that "Japanese" efficiency might be stimulated by higher wages. But, if the original difference has been at all large and the "American" demand is not quite abnormal, the change in relative costs will be the predominant factor. With "Japanese" rates at the "American" level, many branches of "Japanese" industry will be unable to compete. "Japanese" goods will be at a disadvantage, both in "American" and "Japanese" markets. The "Japanese" balance of trade will become unfavourable. There will be a drain of gold to "America". If the regulation is not speedily relaxed, then, as before, there will be unemployment and depression in "Japan", a boom of sorts in "America".

It is obvious that in each case the effects of equalization have been productive of disequilibrium. Let us push the enquiry a stage further and enquire more precisely who benefits. We may confine our attention to the case in which "Japanese" rates are levelled up; the earlier case, in which "American" rates are levelled down, being only of interest as serving to demonstrate, in conjunction with the latter, the essential rôle of the movement of *relative* costs in both instances. Who is it who really gains?

So far as the "Japanese" are concerned there is little benefit. If there are any "Japanese" workmen still left in employment their real incomes will be higher. But if the disparity of rates between our hypothetical " Japan " and " America " is anything like what it is between the Japan and America of reality, presumably there will be very few workmen still in employment. Everyone else will be impoverished in a general deflationary chaos.

The position in " America " is a little more complicated. Obviously " American " consumers are no better off—to put it mildly. " Japanese " imports have increased in price. The prospect of getting some things cheaper from " Japan " than from home sources, which was the occasion of the protest of the producers, has been shattered. There is no special benefit for free capital and labour. If incomes rise with the inflowing gold from " Japan ", prices rise also.

There is, however, one group which benefits. The situation has been saved for the owners of fixed capital in those industries which were menaced by " Japanese " competition. The value of their capital has been preserved. If there are any workers whose skill has become so specialized to the processes of production in these industries that they would be difficult to place elsewhere, they too are in a similar position. There will be no permanent advantage of this sort as this generation of workers retires. For, on our assumptions, given time, it is as easy for workers to

CH. VII WAGES AND HOURS OF LABOUR 165

specialize in one type of industry as in another. Only the very specific factors of production therefore have an advantage.

So that what it all really amounts to is this. There is secured a sectional advantage for the owners of certain factors of production in the high-wage country and some very perilous gains for those workers who remain in employment in the low-wage country. For the rest, in both countries there is loss. The original relation of prices and costs showed that some of the high-wage country's capital and labour would produce more in value terms, if it were put to producing export goods to exchange for "Japanese" imports, than if it continued to produce what it was then producing. It showed too that there was a possible advantage for the low-wage country's capital and labour in an extension of "American" demand for their products. The equalization of wage rates prevents these benefits from accruing. The free factors employed in those of the high-wage country's industries which were threatened by competition were saved the necessity of transfer. But as consumers they suffer with the rest. Only the fixed factors are saved from loss. The rest suffer. From the humanitarian point of view, the frustration of the intentions of the policy is particularly conspicuous in the case of the low-wage country. For, short of permitting migration from one area to another, the right way to raise the standard of living in this country without causing unemployment is to bring about an increase of demand for its products, that is to say, for the services of its factors of production. But the policy we are discussing has done exactly the reverse of this. It has raised the price of one of the factors and thus caused a falling-off of demand. In this respect at least, its effects are not fundamentally dissimilar from the effects of protective duties.

3. But what happens if there is no regulation ? It will facilitate our general enquiry if we push the analysis a little further. Will not the inhabitants of " America " be hopelessly ruined ? Will not their standard of life be reduced to the " Japanese " level ?

Not at all. Let us assume as " unfavourable " a case as can possibly be imagined. Let us assume that there is not one single commodity produced in " America " which can compete at present prices with the " Japanese " products either at home or in " Japan ". And let us assume that " American " consumers buy relentlessly from the cheapest sellers.

What happens ? " America " has imported from " Japan " a volume of goods which has to be paid for. But at present prices " Japan " is not importing from " America ". " American " imports cannot be paid for by " American " exports. It is necessary, therefore, to pay for them in gold.

CH. VII WAGES AND HOURS OF LABOUR 167

Accordingly gold flows out of "America" into "Japan".

But what does this imply? As gold flows out of "America", if conditions are competitive, prices and money incomes fall. As it flows into "Japan", prices and money incomes rise. Eventually a point must be reached when some "American" products are cheap enough to attract "Japanese" purchasers and some "Japanese" products are no longer cheaper to American consumers than the corresponding domestic commodities. "American" exports rise, "Japanese" exports fall. Equilibrium is reached when imports and exports on either side are in such a relation as to obviate the flow of gold. The factors of production in both areas now concentrate on the production of commodities in which their costs of production are lowest. Money incomes in "America" have fallen. But the prices of "American" produce have fallen too; and the commodities purchased from "Japan" are cheaper than they could be made at home. Save in the case of the owners of the specific factors of production, "Americans" are better off. As for "Japan", internal prices will have risen. But so have money incomes, and the commodities purchased from "America" are cheaper than they could be made at home. The "Japanese", too, therefore, are better off. The division of labour has been extended. Real incomes on each side are higher.¹

But there is no reason to suppose that, in such an equilibrium, either real incomes or money incomes are *equal*. The view that advantageous trade between different areas is impossible if wage rates in the different areas are not equal, is in fact completely fallacious. It is possible to speak with great confidence here : this is not one of the propositions upon which there exists any fundamental difference of opinion among competent economists. So long as migration is not completely free, there is no reason whatever to expect that, in conditions of equilibrium, wage rates in different national areas will be equal. Indeed if they are equal it will be a pure accident, just as it would be a pure accident if the level of water in two unconnected vessels were also to happen to be equal.

The reason for this is simple. The wages of the labour employed in any line of production must be paid out of what is received from the sale of the product. Now, when two groups of producers exchange products, there is no reason what-

---

[1] The argument has been based upon the assumption that an orthodox gold standard is in operation and that the supply of gold is fixed. The same conclusion would be reached on the (more realistic) assumption that the supply of gold was increasing but that the whole increase went to " Japan ". The important thing is the shift in *relative* incomes. The same conclusion would be reached, also, on the assumption that in each area there was an inconvertible paper currency. In such a case fluctuations of the rate of exchange would perform the function performed in our example by gold flows and fluctuations of relative prices and money incomes.

CH. VII WAGES AND HOURS OF LABOUR 169

ever to believe that the sums of the prices received, less other expenses (rents, raw materials, etc.), will be such as to afford equal wages on both sides. We should only expect this, if the workers in each group were of exactly equal skill at either line of production and if it was open to them to produce either product under equally advantageous conditions. If this was so, then, of course, if the sum of the prices (less expenses) of one product afforded a poorer wage than the sum of the prices (less expenses) of the other, we should expect a transfer. We should expect some of the labourers to transfer their services from the poorer-paid work to the better, until by the diminution of the supply of the one product and the increase of the supply of the other, the prices were in such a relation as to afford equal pay for equal work. But, of course, in the present condition of the world, it would be absurd to expect such conditions. Labour in different areas is not necessarily of equal skill. And, even if it is, the conditions under which it has to work in the different areas, the margins at which it exploits the natural resources and equipment, may be different. If migration is not possible, there is no reason at all to expect to find labourers of equal skill working at the same margin in different countries. Hence there is no reason to expect to find that the receipts of sales (less expenses) will be such as to produce equality of wage rates. We should all recognize this if the different products were produced and sold by co-operative groups of producers in the different countries. No one would expect the sum of the prices of, say, butter produced in a New Zealand co-operative to yield an income to the New Zealand producer equal to the incomes derived from the sum of the prices of, shall we say, olives produced by co-operatives in Italy. Speaking broadly, the position is not altered substantially by the fact that, in many cases, producers do not earn their incomes as a residue of the excess of receipts over sales but are paid under wage contract at rates fixed before the product is sold.

It follows, therefore, that, so long as migration is not free, we should not expect to find, even under conditions of complete trading equilibrium, an equality of wages or wage rates in different national areas. Leaving on one side altogether differences of skill (which notoriously play a great part in practice), we should expect to find labourers of the same skill working at different margins for different wage rates in different countries. We should expect, too, that most attempts to regulate away such differences would be conducive to disequilibrium and disturbance of the division of labour. When conditions within the different areas are not fully competitive, there may exist small margins within which advances of wages can be brought about merely at the

CH. VII WAGES AND HOURS OF LABOUR 171

expense of profits without modification of output.[1] But speaking broadly, our conclusion holds. Without migration, the conditions of international equilibrium involve no equality of wage rates.

But it follows too that, if wage rates are different, we ought not to expect to find the same types of commodities necessarily produced in all the different areas. Here we come upon a misapprehension not infrequent on the free-trade platforms. Confronted with the demand for the exclusion of competing foreign imports, the overzealous free-trader is apt to argue as if it were only inefficiency on the part of the domestic producers which could ever be the cause of their displacement by foreign competition. How often, for instance, do we hear it said that, if British farmers would only look to their methods of production, they would have nothing to fear from the competition of cheap foreign imports.

This is a most dangerous argument. Of course, there is nearly always something wrong somewhere: and it may happen to be the case that the particular set of producers in question is unusually backward in the adoption of methods of production which are equally accessible and equally profitable to producers any-

---

[1] It is perhaps worth noting that when wage increases are brought about at the expense of an unduly inflated profit margin, the international competitive position is not substantially modified. It is only if " Japanese " labour costs were forced up *in such a way as to affect prices* that "Japanese" competition would be diminished.

where.[1] In such circumstances the accusation is justified. But they may not be inefficient at all. It may simply be that changes in the relative prices of the factors of production at home and elsewhere, make it more advantageous to import the commodity in question and to devote the domestic factors of production to other uses. The decline in the acreage under wheat in England in the latter part of the nineteenth century was certainly not predominantly due to inefficiency on the part of the English wheat farmers. It was simply due to the fact that the prices of land and labour elsewhere made it more profitable for English labour to be devoted to making export goods with which to purchase wheat from abroad than to continue to produce so much wheat at home at a less productive margin. If different types or grades of natural resources can be utilized in the production of similar commodities in different countries, then, even with different wage rates, there may still be some produced in each, with labour at different margins. Thus, in some countries, wheat is grown by comparatively high-paid labour at margins of high productivity, while in others it is grown by low-paid labour at margins of low productivity. But, in so far as similar factors are involved in the

[1] It is not at all clear that the "special correspondents" of great political dailies, who usually "expose" this type of industrial inefficiency, are particularly competent judges. Usually, indeed, their qualifications are almost completely bogus.

production of similar commodities, then, under free trade, differences of wage costs would bring it about that the different industries became concentrated wholly in the centres in which their respective costs of production were least.

Indeed, if we reflect on the matter, we must realize that it is just by such displacements of particular local industries that the international division of labour comes about. As we have seen already, because there are differences in costs of production it is advantageous that the inhabitants of different areas should specialize in those forms of production at which they are comparatively most efficient.[1] Because these differences in costs lead to differences in profits, under free competition, the factors of production in each area are forced out of the lines in which they are relatively less efficient into the lines in which they are relatively more efficient. The latter lines of production are profitable : the former show a loss. If each area could retain types of all industries within its own borders, there would be no international division of labour and none of the advantages which spring therefrom. The notion that, for international competition to be fair, costs of production in the different areas should be equalized is completely without foundation. If costs of production in the different areas were equal, there would be no advantage in trade.

[1] See Chapter III, paras. 2 and 3, above.

4. Let us now make our hypothetical world one degree closer to reality. Hitherto we have been assuming that the world is divided into two areas only. The effects of the regulations we have assumed have, therefore, been confined to the trade between these two areas. Now let us assume also that there exists a third country, let us call it " India ", in whose markets the products of " America " and " Japan " are also in competition. Let us assume that the " American " producers find that they are being undersold by the " Japanese " *in the " Indian " markets.* And let us assume, as before, that on appeal an international tribunal decides that " Japanese " wages must be raised to the " American " level. What happens ?

So far as " Japan " is concerned the position is, broadly speaking, as in the earlier example. " Japanese " costs are raised : and it is more difficult to sell at a profit. There will be unemployment and distress in the " Japanese " export industries, a drain of gold from the " Japanese " financial centres.

But so far as " America " is concerned the position is to some extent different. The " Japanese " competition of which complaint was made was a competition in *export markets.* The beneficiaries of the low costs of production in " Japan " were not " Americans " but consumers in " India ". It is quite possible, therefore, that an extension of

CH. VII WAGES AND HOURS OF LABOUR 175

demand in " India " for the products of " Japan ", while benefiting " India ", might be detrimental to the incomes of producers in general in " America ". There is nothing in the theory of international trade which obliges us to believe that the inhabitants of one area may not be damaged by a transfer of demand for its products to the products of some other area. Indeed Mill's celebrated propositions concerning two countries competing in a third make it expressly clear that this is not so. It is quite possible, then, that the effect of the crippling of the " Japanese " producers by the levelling-up of wages, while obviously detrimental both to the inhabitants of " India " and of " Japan ", may be beneficial to the inhabitants of " America ". It would be as though the " Indians " had imposed a tariff which discriminated against the "Japanese" in favour of the "Americans". It is not certain that this will be so. In so far as direct exchange between "Japan" and "America" was also affected there would be losses to be set against the gains. Still, the thing is conceivable, and in certain cases it is even probable.

In all this, however, there is nothing fundamentally new. In the first example we considered, where it was merely a case of exchange between " America " and " Japan ", we saw that in so far as the " American " factors of production whose industry was menaced by " Japanese " competition were so specialized to the line of production in which they were that they could not be put to other use without loss, then there was obvious gain for them in measures which limited that competition. In the case we are considering here, the whole collection of "American" factors of production are to be regarded as being in something like the same sort of position. Internationally they are relatively specific. If the costs of their competitors in other markets are raised, then their incomes and the value of their capital may be preserved. In each case, the general division of labour has been arrested in the interest of particular groups of producers. In each case, the interests of the many have been sacrificed to the interests of the few.

This result is no accident of the examples which we have chosen. It is the result which we should find whenever and wherever it is attempted to equalize the price of labour, or indeed the prices of any kind of factor of production, without bringing it about that the values of its products are equal.[1] If the different kinds of labour were free to migrate, then there would be a transfer from margins of low productivity to margins of high productivity. In the long run, any wage differences which remained would be due either to

[1] It is an interesting exercise to speculate upon the results of a policy attempting to equalize land rents "in order that competition may be fair".

differences of efficiency or differences in the attractiveness of work. But if, by reason of limitations on movement, the same kinds of labour are compelled to work at different margins in different areas, then the value of their products will not be equal : and attempts to force an equalization of rates of remuneration will generally mean that the division of labour is restricted and the position of those working at inferior margins is even worse than it otherwise need be.

To allow wage rates to approach equality by allowing migration and redistribution of population would make possible a higher volume of production (measured in price terms) than is possible with the same population distributed at points of unequal productivity. But to equalize wage rates without thus equalizing the productivity of labour is to make impossible even that volume of production of which the maldistributed populations is capable.

5. Very similar reasoning is applicable to proposals for the international equalization, not of wages, but of hours of labour.[1]

---

[1] It should be observed in what follows that the analysis is directed only to the effects of *equalization* of hours. [I have analysed the effects of general reduction of hours in the *Great Depression*, chap. vii. para. 2, and (with more technical detail) in " The Economic Effects of Variations of Hours of Labour ", *Economic Journal*, vol. xli. pp. 25-40.] The analysis of this section is perhaps rather more technical than that of other parts of the chapter and it may be omitted without loss of continuity.

It should be clear that, in most cases, an equalization of the length of the working day all round to the standard of the advanced areas would lower productivity per day in the areas in which the day was longer. If the day were the wrong side of the production optimum, that is, if it were so long that more would be produced if it were shortened, of course this would not happen. But it has not been shown that this optimum is usually exceeded. For if it were so, then producers in the areas in which hours were longer would have a competitive advantage if hours were shortened. It is safe to assume that proposals for the equalization of hours of labour are not usually intended to shift the ratio of costs *against* producers in the short-day areas !

If productivity per day is reduced and wages are adjusted to the resulting change in the value of output, the net effect is likely to be some lowering of the real incomes of the workers affected, by way of a reduction of money incomes, and some lowering of the real incomes of their customers, by way of some increase in the price of their products. It is possible that a reduction in output might so raise the world price of their product as to more than counterbalance the effect of a reduction in the number of units sold : in such a case the real incomes of the producers would rise. But where the local output is highly competitive with output from other areas this is very improbable. Much more likely is a diminution in the total value of local output such that, in order that full employment may be preserved, a downward revision of incomes is necessary.

If, however, wages are not adjusted to variations in productivity, then the effect of lower productivity per day will be an upward movement of cost per unit. If local costs rise relatively to costs elsewhere as a result of such a lowering of productivity, then the competitive position of the producers in question is likely to be impaired. The position is not quite the same as it would be with wage equalization : for some relative variation in local productivity is here given by hypothesis, and hence there must also be some immediate change in equilibrium prices. But it is extremely improbable that any favourable movement of the prices per unit of the output of the areas where productivity has been lowered will offset the obviously unfavourable movement of costs. Hence the main outlines of our earlier analysis hold. The position of the producers whose costs have been raised, is worsened. The position of consumers of their goods is worsened also. The gainers are solely those factors of production whose remuneration stood to be lowered by the more successful service of the consuming public by their competitors. Not without justice do the representatives at international conferences of the low wage, long-day areas look askance at proposals from elsewhere that they should reduce hours to levels prevailing abroad. For the chief beneficiaries of such proposals would be groups of producers immediately menaced by their competition. The chief losers would be themselves. And the volume of production as a whole would be reduced.

We can perhaps best see the differences and the similarities between the equalization of hours and the equalization of wages if we examine an hypothesis, similar in its practical remoteness to the hypothesis with which we commenced the examination of wage equalization. Let us suppose that, competition from " backward " (*i.e.* poorer) areas being acute, it is proposed to equalize hours by international regulation. But let us suppose that, instead of hours in the " backward " areas being reduced, it is decreed that hours shall be increased elsewhere. Let us ignore the obvious political complications which would accompany so absurd a policy and enquire solely concerning its economic implications.

Obviously the position as regards the amount of work done would be different from what it would be if hours in the " backward " areas were reduced. Our example here shows no symmetry with the case of wage equalization. The crude volume of production would be greater. But it would be increased by forced labour. There is no reason to suppose that, even in the absence of

CH. VII   WAGES AND HOURS OF LABOUR   181

legislation regarding hours of labour, labourers in "advanced" countries would wish to work as long as labourers in the "backward" countries.

But as regards *relative* costs of production the position would be broadly the same as in the case of equalization by reduction. That is to say, if hours were increased in the advanced countries and no adjustments made in daily wages, then the competitive position of the "backward" producers would be worsened. It is unlikely, however, that this would mean a reduction of real incomes in the "backward" areas, save for the owners of factors of production specific to the lines of production whose competitive power was diminished. For by hypothesis the advanced areas would be working for the rest of the world on cheaper terms: and the non-specific factors in the "backward" areas would merely have to specialize in other lines of production to be actually better off. But, as regards relative costs, the symmetry with the case of equalization by reduction remains instructive.

The fact is that leisure, that is to say, freedom from work, is an ingredient of real income equally with the necessities, comforts and luxuries which we enjoy during our leisure. It is purchased by the sacrifice of the other ingredients of real income which we might have produced if we had devoted more of our fixed supply of twenty-four hours per day to activities other than leisure. The amount that we actually purchase will depend, partly upon our valuation of leisure, partly upon our capacity to produce the other ingredients of real income with which we purchase it. We should not expect all men to work equal hours even if they were all equally productive. If they are not equally productive, then *a fortiori* we should not expect equality. As we have seen, to enforce equality by compelling a reduction of the hours of the poorer is, at best, if wages are flexible, to make them (and those to whom they sell their products) poorer than before. If wages are rigid, so that costs are out of harmony with productivity, then still further disharmonies are likely to be introduced.

6. If the analysis of this chapter is correct, it follows that the whole notion of making possible an orderly international co-operation by the equalization of wages and hours of labour falls to the ground. The project of achieving in this way the double aim of removing the causes of international anarchy and the injustice of international inequality was based upon misconception.

This conclusion is sincerely to be regretted. But it does not seem possible to evade it. Once it is realized that real incomes are conditioned by the productivity and the relative desire for leisure of labour, and that relative costs are simply part of a market mechanism which shows how best the inhabitants of the different areas

CH. VII WAGES AND HOURS OF LABOUR 183

may earn their real incomes, the belief that equality may be successfully imposed without equalizing tastes and productivity is seen to rest on delusion. It is a delusion to which the accidental circumstances of the wage system, with its division between the market for products and the market for services, may appear to lend some countenance. But it is a delusion nevertheless : and it is a delusion by whose aid the vested interests, both of capital and of labour, are enabled to divert attention from the real causes of geographical inequality, the limitations on trade and on migration, and to construct on the misconceptions of men of goodwill new defences for their positions of monopoly.[1]

[1] It should be noted that the argument of this chapter is concerned essentially with the relationship of wages aud hours in different areas rather than with their absolute level. It is important to realize this. The disagreements concerning wages and the volume of employment which have recently developed among economists relate essentially to absolute wages. The broad outlines of the theory of relative wages are not the subject of serious controversy. Professional economists will observe that, for the most part, I have here relegated considerations of certain possible " terms of trade " complications to parenthetical clauses and certain reservations of statement : in a more detailed study, these would come in for more explicit survey. But for the purposes of this chapter, the analysis of the broad effects of general wage equalization, etc., it is submitted that such treatment is unnecessary.

PART III

COMPLETE INTERNATIONAL PLANNING

CHAPTER VIII

INTERNATIONAL COMMUNISM

1. WE have now reached a new stage in our argument. In the first part we examined independent national planning. We found that it led to results which were highly unsatisfactory. In the second part, therefore, we were led to examine certain forms of planning on international lines which it was hoped would remove these deficiences—the planning of particular channels of trade, particular lines of production, and of the relationship of wages and hours of labour. But we found no solution in these directions. The plans we examined all proved, in the last analysis, to be infected with sectional interest and to lead to an "uneconomical" use of resources. They all considered the parts by themselves rather than the relation of the parts in the whole. It is natural, therefore, that we should now turn to consider plans of a more comprehensive nature. In this part we shall be concerned with international planning of the entire field of production, distribution and exchange.

2. Let us start with international communism —a totalitarian plan for the world. Let us suppose that there exists an international authority owning and disposing of all the natural resources, all the artificial equipment in existence. Let us suppose too that it is the sole employer of labour. On what principles would it plan its productive operations?

It is obvious that we are now to discuss something which, at the moment at any rate, is far less practicable than anything we have hitherto analysed. International communism is not yet practical politics. It is not likely to become so for many years to come. But the idea of international communism is, even now, one of the driving forces of practical politics. It is a hope which actuates an increasing number of the world's inhabitants. And even if it has often been propagated by appeal to motives of hatred and revenge, it must surely be admitted to be, in itself, an idea which is impressive and admirable, deserving of the most eager, the most scrupulous attention. The idea of communism is both rationalist and utilitarian. If we reject it, it must be, not because we reject the ends it seeks, but because we find the means it proposes unsuitable for attaining their object.

Unfortunately in examining such proposals, we labour under a certain disadvantage. Although the main presumption of complete international

CH. VIII INTERNATIONAL COMMUNISM   189

communism—central ownership of the means of production, distribution and exchange—has been the subject of ceaseless propaganda for nearly a hundred years, very few attempts have been made to show how such a plan would work. The early communists, it is true, planned out in some detail the small self-contained communities which they proposed to establish. But the Marxian analysis dismissed all such speculations as "Utopian". It was declared to be waste of time to investigate how the system in whose favour the existing institutions of society were to be violently destroyed would actually work in practice. The coming of socialism was inevitable. It was implicit in the whole process of historical development. All that the communist could usefully do was, by agitation and propaganda, to endeavour to shorten the "pangs" of the period of transition. The people to whom they addressed their propaganda, therefore, were rather in the position of those who, at the time of the South Sea Bubble, were asked to subscribe to "a project the nature of which will be hereafter disclosed". It is the startling fact that in the whole range of socialist literature, constituting a library of very many thousands of items, until a few years ago there was no systematic discussion of the most elementary economic problems confronting a society which was completely socialist. Socialists of the Fabian type were content with minute projects for the socialization of particular municipal or national lines of industry. The communists proper definitely ruled out such speculations as the product of bourgeois intellectual habits.

In recent years, however, largely as a result of the work of von Mises and Max Weber, it has been gradually realized that there are problems here which need solution. It has been realized that speculations about the socialization of particular industries in a capitalist society do not even begin to touch the problem of the mutual relations of the different parts of the economic system when all industry is socialized; that in fact this is *the* problem of complete international socialism : that until it is solved we cannot entertain any confidence that, if we could achieve such a system tomorrow, we should have exchanged a worse society for a better. It is one of the hopeful signs of recent years that a few of the younger socialists have commenced to discuss this problem in a scientific manner. But it would be wrong to say that any commonly agreed solution has been reached, even in the broadest outline. It cannot yet be regarded as proved that world socialism can work in such a way as to do what is expected of it. It is true, therefore, to say that the millions of people for whom socialism is the chief hope of existence, like the countless multitudes who in earlier ages have placed their trust in other forms of mass belief, live on faith rather than on logical demonstration. Somewhere, sometime, they think, intelligent and disinterested men have thought it all out. . . . But unfortunately this is not true.

3. Let us see whether this demonstration cannot be accomplished.

We may assume throughout our investigation that the object of the plan is to provide for the wants of the citizens. We will assume too that the citizens are regarded as being themselves the best judges of what they want.

This last is perhaps a perilous assumption. The rulers of this world have not often regarded their subjects as being the best judges of their own happiness. In our own day, there are many who would willingly dictate to their fellows the way they should live and act. There is certainly some danger that the mechanism of a centralized world state, more powerful for the suppression of freedom than anything the world has yet seen, would gravitate into the hands of such distasteful types. To adapt the people to the plan rather than the plan to the people is not likely to cease to be a temptation. But it is assumed here that planning of this sort would be so repugnant to any to whom it is hoped that this book may appeal that its more detailed implications are not worth discussing. The only type of plan which is regarded as acceptable here is the plan which seeks to adapt the organization of production to the free choices of the citizens.

But how is this to be done ? Two things are clearly necessary. On the one hand, there must be a mechanism for ascertaining wants. On the other hand, there must be a mechanism which organizes production according to these requirements. Let us look at these separately.

A mechanism for ascertaining the wants of the citizens is not at all difficult to imagine. It is obvious that such a mechanism would be necessary. The wants of the two thousand million inhabitants of the world could not be sympathetically interpreted in a government office, in the same way as the wants of a small family may (sometimes) be sympathetically and disinterestedly interpreted by the head of the household. It is obvious, too, that the mechanism of political election would be inappropriate. Political elections, if they concern not men but issues, must relate to a single decision : and the alternative possibilities of production on a world scale are not single but multitudinous. If our consumption is really to be *à la carte* and not a comprehensive take-it-or-leave-it *table d'hôte*—to use one of Mr. Schwartz's significant metaphors—choice has to be made day by day, not merely between sausages and eggs-and-bacon, but between a little more or a little less of all the almost infinite combinations of the possible ingredients of real income. A

CH. VIII   INTERNATIONAL COMMUNISM   193

general election every day would be needed, and a general election not on one but millions of possible issues. And even then the decisions would be the decisions of unweighted majorities.

Fortunately, however, there exists a mechanism which is subject to none of these deficiencies. If the consumers are provided with money and allowed to bid for the different commodities available, the result of their bidding will be to establish, as it were, a scale of social valuations. Each individual is at liberty to distribute his expenditure in such a way that he cannot gain by transferring money from one commodity to another. The prices in the markets are the resultant of this process of individual valuation. Naturally the system is not perfect. If the incomes of the citizens are not equal—and even under complete communism there is reason to suppose some differences in efficiency wages—then the voters have, as it were, unequal votes. If incomes are equal, there is no reason to suppose that capacity for enjoyment is equal—whatever that may be conceived to mean. But as a means of ascertaining preferences, *given the distribution of income*, the market is incomparably superior to any other that has ever been suggested. It gives free play to individual idiosyncrasy. It affords constant information concerning changes in individual idiosyncrasy. It permits, as it were, a perpetual referendum, with due weight for minorities, on all the possible issues which concern the sphere of private consumption.

4. Let us suppose, then, that the wants of the citizens are ascertained in this way. In what way will the planning authorities proceed to organize production so as to satisfy these wants as well as possible ? [1]

Let us first be quite clear as to the task they have to perform. We know that a consumer has planned his expenditure rationally when his outlay of money on the different things he can buy is such that, if he were to transfer a unit of expenditure from one to another, the things that he would gain would give him less satisfaction than the things he would lose. Similarly, if he is working for himself as a producer, he will plan rationally if he so distributes his working time between the different things he can do that to work a little less at one thing and a little more at another would mean that he gained less than he lost.

The same criteria are applicable to social planning. Society as a whole does not buy anything. But there is labour available which can be used in many ways. There are machines, raw materials, natural resources which may be used in many lines of production. The criterion of suc-

---

[1] The next two sections owe much to the work of Professor von Mises. A fuller treatment of many of the points touched on will be found in the various essays in Professor Hayek's *Collectivist Economic Planning*.

cessful social planning, therefore, is that production is organized in such a way that none of the available factors of production can be withdrawn from what they are actually doing and put to uses which are more valuable, in terms of the prices of the commodities which they might produce. Each unit of each of the different kinds of labour, each unit of the different types of land, each unit of the different kinds of raw materials, etc., must be used in a way which secures the highest return in price terms. In this way the preferences of the citizens expressed in terms of money are satisfied as fully as possible in the given situation. It is not to be expected that any organization will satisfy the criterion completely. If the choices of the consumers change, if the natural conditions of production alter, or if technical knowledge improves, at any moment there must always be some disparity between the actual and the "ideal" distribution of resources. Our judgment of the success of any organization therefore must be based, not on its capacity at any moment to achieve the "ideal", but upon its capacity continually to *tend* in that direction.

Now this is not an engineering problem, although it is often thought to be so. The planning authority will not be able to decide the allocation of its resources by calling in the engineers. No doubt in deciding how best to produce *any particular commodity* the advice of the engineers will be indispensable. A knowledge of the potentialities of various techniques is essential for successful planning. But in deciding *whether to produce this commodity or that, or in what proportions to produce both, the technique of the engineers is helpless.* It is an economic, not a technical problem. And even in the decision how best to produce particular commodities, engineering information is only one part of the solution.

A simple illustration should make this clear. Let us suppose that the planning authority has decided to produce a certain extra quantity of, shall we say, wheat. How will it decide in what part of the world to produce it ? At first sight it might seem as if this were essentially an engineering problem. Agricultural experts should be asked to indicate that part where the fertility of the soil and the efficiency of labour is the greatest. Where else would it be rational that the new enterprise should be located ?

But, as we have already seen in another connection,[1] this would be a bad mistake. The parts of the world most fertile for wheat production might quite easily be parts which, if devoted to some other purpose, would produce a higher return in value terms. In such a case it would be uneconomical to use such land for wheat-growing. Economy would consist in growing the wheat elsewhere ! The criterion of a rational plan is not

[1] Chapter III, para. 2, above.

that different commodities should be produced by the instruments most efficient for producing them, but that the different instruments should be each used to produce those things which have the highest value. This is not a problem of engineering technique at all. It is a problem of computing costs—a problem of deciding what would be sacrificed *in value terms* if the land were devoted to growing wheat rather than, shall we say, the production of asparagus, or providing a site for a factory. It is a problem of valuation, of comparing products which are physically unlike. There is no measuring-rod in the engineer's tool-bag which can accomplish the comparison. " Which is more ," we used to be asked when we were children, " a hundred elephants or seventy bags of wheat ? " To ask engineers, *as engineers*, to tell us how to distribute the different factors of production between their different possible uses is to ask a similar nonsense question. Only economic calculation, not in physical but in value terms, can solve the problem of social planning.

Now there can be no doubt that this problem can be solved fairly satisfactorily without any elaborate mechanism by an isolated producer working for himself, or by the head of a small patriarchal community. The various alternatives of production can be surveyed and compared by a more or less direct method of valuation. " If we devote an extra hour per day to hoeing, we sacrifice the opportunity of spending that time in hunting or ditching or building new shelters against the weather . . ." they may say. It should not be difficult to judge which mode of work will yield the highest return.

But we are not thinking of the organization of an isolated farm or a small patriarchal community. We are thinking of the possibilities of organizing the productive activities of hundreds of millions of human beings, disposing of world-wide stocks of different kinds of material resources, with an almost infinite range of possibilities of productive techniques. We are thinking of the co-ordination of the uses of the resources of five continents and the occupational distribution of the working population of the world. It is obvious that the methods of direct inspection, satisfactory enough in the small community, are completely inappropriate here. Some measuring-rod, some impersonal mode of calculating costs, is necessary if the thing is not to be completely arbitrary. It is not enough to know the preferences of the consumers. We must also know the costs which are incurred by different modes of satisfying these preferences.

Now, if the various factors of production had prices which were each a reflection of the value of the products which they were each capable of producing, the process of planning would be simple. The planning authority would compare the costs of producing commodities with the prices they secured in the market. If, in any line of production, cost was less than price, they would know that production there should be extended. If it were greater than price, then production there should be contracted. If the price of wheat in any part, for instance, was greater than the cost of producing it there, then the production of wheat should be extended; for the value of the other things which could be produced from the land and labour required for producing wheat would be less than the value of the wheat. If it were less, then wheat production should be contracted; for the factors employed in producing wheat could produce a greater value doing something else. If the factors of production had prices which were equal to the value of their specific products or were continually likely to tend to be equal, the problem would be solved.

But here is the paradox of the situation. If the factors of production are owned and controlled from the centre, a market in which they are priced no longer exists. A market involves buyers and sellers. If the instruments of production, the land, the labour, the raw materials and semimanufactures are all under one central control, the market is of necessity eliminated. To plan centrally on a world scale demands a measure— a common denominator to which the various technical potentialities of production can be assimilated. But to control centrally destroys the apparatus by which such a measure is established. Without prices for the factors of production, the planning authority cannot tell whether it is disposing of its resources so as best to meet the wants of the consumers.

At first sight it may seem as if there were an easy way out of this difficulty. As we have seen, the cost of producing a commodity is to be regarded as the value of what is sacrificed by not using the resources in question to produce something else. Now the market for consumers' goods may be conceived to indicate the consumers' preferences for the different things which can be produced. The engineers can tell us what given quantities of the factors of production are capable of producing in their different uses. We know how many factors of production are available. Can we not combine this information in such a way as to calculate costs of production?

Calculations of this sort are certainly conceivable. Mathematical economics indeed shows us how, given much the same items of information as we have noted above (the consumers' preferences, the technical coefficients of production and the supplies of the factors of production), the appropriate prices for the factors of production and their distribution between different uses may be discovered by the solution of a series of simultaneous equations. But the same mathematical propositions enable us to see how practically impossible it would be to assemble and to manipulate the information necessary. It would be necessary to know, not merely the actual prices of the different commodities available, given the supply actually on the market, but also the potentialities of price variation, given changes in these supplies. It would be necessary to know the possibilities of producing each possible commodity with each possible combination of productive resources. And, given all this complicated and inaccessible information, it would be necessary to solve the simultaneous equations resulting therefrom. It is safe to say that, once the number of commodities involved exceeds a comparatively small number, the operations, both of ascertaining the relevant information and manipulating it in a suitable way, would be quite impracticable. In a world economy, with hundreds of thousands of types of commodities and hundreds of thousands of ways of producing them, the attainment of one solution, let alone the continuous change of solution which changing conditions would involve, would be completely out of the question.[1]

It is easy to form false views about this matter by over-simplifying our conceptions of the nature of the actual processes of production. If the only

---

[1] See the classical treatment of this subject in Barone, *The Ministry of Production in the Collectivist State*, reprinted in Hayek, *Collectivist Economic Planning*.

factor of production were unskilled labour, then we could reckon costs in units of labour. Then if the price of any commodity were not in harmony with its labour cost of production, its production would have to be contracted or extended.[1] Or if each type of commodity were made by processes, each involving the use of only one of the different types of factors of production, as, for instance, simple spinning operations by female labour, simple fencing by male labour, it might not be so difficult to make lists of the different commodities which each factor of production could produce and thus to discover, by reference to market prices and conjectures regarding changes of such prices, in which line lay the highest return.

But these assumptions are highly unrealistic. There is not one type of factor of production, unskilled labour ; there are many. There are many types of labour, many types of material resources. In so far as they are scarce, they all need to be economized : their use in one line of production involves sacrifices elsewhere which should enter into the computation of costs. The different types of productive processes do not use the various factors of production singly ; almost every process involves the use of more than one kind of factor of production ; not only labour but

[1] It is possible that a vague belief that labour reckoning was sufficient to solve the value problem was at the basis of some, at least, of the apparent lack of interest in this problem on the part of the early socialists.

CH. VIII   INTERNATIONAL COMMUNISM   203

land and raw materials, not one kind of labour and land and raw materials but many. Moreover the proportions in which they are combined are not fixed but can be varied according to the availability of the different factors. If land is scarce, wheat can be grown intensively (*i.e.* with little land and much labour). If labour is scarce, it can be grown extensively (with little labour and much land). All of which means that there is no simple method of computing costs. Either the prices of the factors of production must be established by a comprehensive calculation of *all* the possibilities—which, as we have seen, is out of the question—or they must be established in the market by competitive bidding. And this, as we have seen, is ruled out so long as their disposition is decreed *ab initio* from the centre. If the productive operations which have to be planned are on an international scale—and it is this problem we are discussing—then it is safe to say that, if there is no market for the factors of production, there is no method of accurate costing available. And without accurate costing, an economical satisfaction of the wants of the citizens cannot be planned.

Let us be quite clear what this means : for there has been much unnecessary confusion on this subject. It does *not* mean that the planning authority cannot draw up a series of projects. It does *not* mean that these projects cannot be executed. It is perfectly obvious that, given labour and materials and engineering skill, factories and workshops and power stations and so on can be erected and final commodities produced. And there is no reason why, given some means of maintaining output, either by way of rewards or coercion, the different productive units should not be run with some degree of technical efficiency. Nor is there any reason to believe that the products, such as they are, will not satisfy some wants. If a communist state erects a factory for manufacturing boots and the citizens do not possess all the boots they require, then the products of the factory will be acceptable and will command a price in the market.

All this is common ground but it does not meet the root question. The root question is, not whether the factory can be erected and run with technical efficiency, but whether, by using the resources of the community to build this factory and to run it, those resources are being used more fruitfully than they could be used in any other way. If the wants of the consumers are to be satisfied as fully as possible, then the resources of society must not be applied to produce just anything which happens to be scarce and which therefore commands a price. They must be used to produce those things which are more urgently demanded than any others which could be produced if they were put to other uses. This, and this only, is the criterion of rational planning : not merely to use all factors to produce something, but rather to put each factor to the point of highest return. But this, as we have seen, cannot be accomplished on a large scale without prices for the factors of production. And if the market is abolished there can be no prices for the factors of production. Plans may be made and carried out which involve the execution of a vast schedule of technical prescriptions. But, unless these technical prescriptions can be assimilated to a common denominator by an apparatus of valuation—an apparatus of prices and costs—they cannot be said to fulfil what we have postulated to be the object of planning. The consumption of the people adapts itself to the output of the plan, not the output of the plan to the desires as regards consumption of the people.

5. It is probable that at the present time the correctness of the above analysis would be conceded in most circles pretending to technical competence. Ten years ago it would have been vigorously contested. Those who upheld it were reviled and ostracized as reactionaries and incompetents. But today they have won all along the line. Whatever may be the views of politicians and the rank-and-file socialists—and of course, here as elsewhere, there is a time-lag of perhaps fifteen or twenty years in such matters—at the

present day few responsible socialist economists would deny that a planning authority which seeks to plan without the guidance of a price system will be planning without a measure. Nor would they deny that, in a system of world dimensions, a pricing of the factors of production is impracticable without the market. The question to-day is whether an effective market in some shape or form is not possible once private property is abolished. Not whether the market is necessary, but whether the market can be retained![1]

It is often suggested that the problem can be solved by making the different branches of industry quasi-independent units. The different industries are to be organized in separate trusts, responsible in the last resort to the central government. They are to hire their capital from the exchequer and pay their profits to it. But, in their dealings with each other and with the general body of consumers, they are to proceed upon an exchange basis.

It should be clear, from what we have seen in an earlier chapter, that this is a type of policy not out of harmony with developments which have actually taken place in certain important lines of industry and not uncongenial to the type of mind which has been responsible for these developments. If it is desirable that *one* line of industry

[1] See, for instance, Mr. Durbin's "Economic Calculus in a Planned Economy," *Economic Journal*, vol. xlvi, p. 676 *seq.*

should be organized as a unit, is it not desirable that *all* should be organized on the same principle?

But at the same time it is a policy which suffers from most of these deficiencies which we discovered when examining this type of planning particular lines of industry ; and it suffers from yet another which only arises when such planning has become general. It tends to stereotype the *status quo*. It tends to make the prosperity of the different industries, rather than the distribution of resources between industries, the criterion of successful planning. And—and this is the crucial point in this connection—it destroys the competitive market. It is quite possible for government trusts of this sort to conduct their mutual relations on a basis of money reckoning. They can bid against each other for the services of other factors of production. But they do not create competitive prices, either for what they buy or for what they sell. It is a commonplace of price theory that bargaining between such monopolies is indeterminate between wide limits, save in terms of negotiating strategy. Prices are fixed. But they are virtually arbitrary. They are a reflection of power, not productivity. They will not afford a satisfactory basis for the type of planning we want. The "*the* industry" fallacy is no less insidious when its application is completely generalized.

Much more interesting is the suggestion completely to revive a competitive organization of industry. The different industries are to be broken up into small units, no larger than considerations of technical efficiency make absolutely necessary. The ownership of the capital and the means of production on which it is spent are to remain the property of the community : any other plan would clearly be incompatible with the very conception of communism. But the managers are to compete with each other, both in the sale of products and in the purchase of the services of the factors of production. They are to behave *as if* under competitive capitalism. They are, as it were, to *play* at competition. Such proposals are much less likely to be adopted than proposals for all-embracing governmental monopolies. But they show a much firmer grasp of the fundamental problems. At first sight, indeed, they appear to promise the best of both worlds : the advantages of the mechanism of competition, without the disadvantages of the inequalities which are the by-product of the property system on which the mechanism of competition rests at present.

But how would such a system actually work in practice ? It is obviously not the same as the system of free enterprise ; and it is important to be clear exactly wherein the differences consist. The managers of the production units are state servants. The property they administer is not their own property or the property of a group of shareholders. It is the property of the community at large. The community at large therefore assumes the ultimate risk of enterprise. To the community at large flows the profit or loss of the business.

It follows therefore that the principles of management must be bureaucratic. Just because they are servants of the state and the custodians of its property, the managers will be obliged to adopt procedures of record and explicit formulation of the reasons for decisions of policy which are not necessary to anything like the same degree under private enterprise. This is not to say that they will be less able or less zealous than the administrators of private property. The critics of bureaucratic procedure are barking up altogether the wrong tree if they impugn the ability or the zeal of state servants. Experience shows that there is no reason why the standard in these respects should necessarily be inferior to the standards of private business: indeed the contrary is sometimes the case. The reason for the obvious differences between the speed and flexibility of the two types of organization is, not that the civil servant is necessarily inefficient, but that he is responsible to political control. Because he is responsible to political control, because reasons for his actions may be demanded in the sovereign assembly, he must keep records, he must observe precedents, he must abide by rules of procedure. This is not in the least unreasonable. It would be intolerable if a public servant, guaranteed against loss by the public purse, had powers of arbitrary action. But it means that his speed and his initiative are necessarily greatly impeded.

It follows, too—what is more immediately germane to the central problem under discussion—that the scope of competitive action must be confined within certain limits. The managers of the productive units are to sell against each other in the product markets. They are to bid against each other in the markets for factors of production. But it is scarcely to be supposed that they are to be free to change the general use of their capital. As the manager of a communal cotton factory, a government servant may be permitted—even ordered—to undersell his competitors in the market for cotton cloth and to overbid them if necessary in the markets for labour and materials. But can we assume that he is free to transform his business altogether, to become a merchant instead of a manufacturer, or a producer of some other commodity? Is he to be free to close down his works in Lancashire and to commence operations in Japan? The thing is not impossible to conceive. But it is really most improbable in practice.

But if this is not so, then the competitive system is not re-created. For it is the essence of capitalist competition in a changing world that there should be a continual reinvestment of capital in new forms and combinations. The prices of the factors of production are the resultant of changing demand and changing supply. Under static conditions, it is easy enough to conceive of a fictitious competition which might very well sustain an efficiency which might wane under complete centralization. But the main function of the price system is dynamic; and it is difficult to see how dynamic competition can be effectively re-created by any decentralization which stops short of institutions incompatible with central ownership.

Is it not possible that the advocates of these schemes, ingenious and able though they be, are still suffering from a subtle infection of the "*the* industry" fallacy?

6. These doubts are greatly reinforced if we cast our net rather wider. Let us consider the system proposed, not from the point of view of particular production managers, but from a point of view embracing the factor markets in general. And let us keep firmly in mind that we are constructing an *international* system.

It is of the essence of communism that incomes shall be equalized. By this is not excluded the possibility of inequality due to inequalities of output or premiums for special skill and responsibility. It is obvious that, if the system is not to resort to coercion in the day-in day-out conduct of industry, there must exist some adjustment of reward to effort. But the inequality which is allowed must be an inequality due to circumstances for which the individual must be held in greater or less degree responsible. Inequality due to inequality of market position must be held to be quite incompatible with the main principles of the system.

Now, for a communism which is truly international, this presents a problem whose difficulty can scarcely be exaggerated. The distribution of the population of the world as it exists today, and as it is likely to exist under the most favourable conditions for many generations to come, is not such as to equalize the value of the marginal product of the same kind of labour in different places. If we make the widest allowances for differences of capacity, it is still probable that there remain differences of very great magnitude. And the differences of capacity themselves are very real. There is no reason whatever to expect changes which will even approximately equalize the productivity of different people.

But this means that the planning authority is confronted with a dilemma which is truly stupendous. If it decrees equal prices for labour everywhere it substantially falsifies the basis of economic calculation. We have seen already the catastrophic results of policies of international wage equalization. If the price of labour is not in rough equivalence to the value of its product, then one of the main supports of a system of economic calculation is removed. But on the other hand, if the production units are ordered to compete in the labour markets as elsewhere, then the widest disparities of rates of remuneration will emerge. The equalitarian principle of international communism is broken. This is *not* a matter of unequal pay for unequal application. That, as we have seen, may be regarded as likely and permissible. It is a matter of unequal pay for equal application, a matter of high labour incomes in America and low incomes in Russia, of high rates in Australia and low rates in Austria. It is an inequalitarian framework for the operation of the premium system.

But what can be done about it within the limits of communist principle ? Presumably there would be attempted forced transfers of labour on a very extensive scale. But it seems quite unrealistic to suppose that, for many decades to come, such transfers could bring about anything approaching equal productivities. During the time in which the system was proving its worth, this dilemma would continue to confront it. Either equality of rates of remuneration, in which case economic calculations would be seriously falsified : or inequality, in which case the *raison d'être* of the system would be abrogated.

It is sometimes suggested that the difficulty could be met by a system of taxes and subsidies. The managers of the production units would bid for labour according to its productivity and would keep accounts on that basis. But the incomes actually paid out would be equalized by deduction from the " wages " that were higher and subsidies to the " wages " that were less.

The suggestion is ingenious. But it is difficult to believe that its advocates have ever really reflected on the quantitative problem involved. Statistics of global income and production are notoriously unreliable and exactitude is necessarily impossible. But it is still quite certain that, if property incomes were abolished and an international equalization of work incomes attempted, there is hardly a worker in the " advanced " countries whose real income would not be severely diminished. And it is doubtful whether the increase elsewhere would be very considerable. Mankind as a whole is still desperately poor : the abolition of inequality on a world scale, even if it involved no diminution of world production, would do little to raise the average. But one may well ask whether the workers of the advanced countries would stand it. If we consider only a European system, we may still question whether the workers of Sweden, or Great Britain, or even Germany, would willingly submit to a reduction of their incomes to something, perhaps, a little above the Italian level. In Russia this problem is not overwhelming : all start more or less from a common level of absolute poverty. But it would become a political problem of the first order of magnitude were the Russian system extended.

Is it not likely that an international system which was run on these lines would speedily break up into antagonistic units of the Fascist Nationalist type with the consequences that we have already examined ?

7. If we turn to the problem of capital accumulation and capital disposal we reach equally depressing conclusions.

In a system of private property, the act of saving is voluntary. This is not to say that there does not exist " forced saving " brought about by manipulation of the banking system or the system of public finance. But, speaking broadly, capital accumulation depends on the voluntary decisions of private individuals and corporations,[1] saving to a margin of their own choice.

[1] This must not be construed as giving approval to the policy of corporate saving which has become so conspicuous a feature in our day. There is strong reason to suppose that this may often involve considerable waste of resources and rigidity of the capital market. This is one of the many respects in which the present company law is in urgent need of careful scrutiny from the economic point of view.

Under communism, capital accumulation would still be necessary. Not even Mr. Keynes would seriously argue that the opportunities for capital investment in the world as a whole are within sight of being exhausted. Indeed, if the hitherto chronic poverty of the vast majority of the world's inhabitants is ever to be remedied, capital accumulation on a scale quite as large as anything witnessed during the nineteenth century must continue for a very long while. There are hundreds of millions of labourers in the East at present working at margins which afford scarcely the means of subsistence. Not merely birth control but the most extensive capital accumulation would be necessary to change this dreadful condition.

Under communism, however, individual saving would be of quite subordinate importance. The main function of deciding upon capital accumulation would be discharged by the central planning authority. It would consist essentially in a decision to apply a certain proportion of the total resources available to providing the means of real income, not for the present but for the future. As with the individual, it would be a decision to forgo so much now, in the hope of having more in compensation later on.

Now we will not pause to investigate whether, under such a system, more or less would be saved than under capitalistic institutions. It is clearly

INTERNATIONAL COMMUNISM 217

partly a question of the form of government. Dictatorships might compel more saving than under capitalism; effective democracies less. Nor will we discuss further the question whether the mechanism of calculation of such a society would permit a rational allocation of the resources, thus saved, between different forms of production. But it is pertinent for our purposes to observe that, if the productivity per head of different sections of the society is not equal, and if the allocation of the capital resources saved is not equal, a general deduction all round from potential present incomes will involve *unequal* sacrifice. If, for instance, the services of the inhabitants of, say, Scandinavia are in part devoted to providing resources to raise the productivity of the inhabitants of China, that means, as in the case of income equalization, that they get less than they might have had in order that others may get more.

This problem is not an imaginary one. It is a problem which is already exemplified in the history of the Russian System. Whatever be our interpretation of the various plans which have hitherto been attempted within that mysterious country, whether they are to be regarded as primarily preparation for military defence, or attempts to satisfy some ultimate criterion of happiness, it is clear that they have been carried through by the imposition of forced saving on the peasantry. If the peasantry had been permitted to sell their produce on the world market or even at free prices at home, there can be no shadow of doubt that their real incomes would have been higher. There is no doubt, that is to say, that forced saving has been inflicted upon them in the interests of the general plan. This is not the biassed diagnosis of minds out of sympathy with the general nature of the system. It is the diagnosis of communists themselves.[1] And it is a diagnosis which would necessarily fit still more the operations of a more extensive system. No doubt the problem arises in some measure even under capitalist institutions. If the export of capital is prohibited, there may be gain for some groups of wage-earners. But it is a difference in degree almost equivalent to a difference in kind. The initial sacrifice, such as it is, is the sacrifice of the savers : and the interests in this respect of the different groups of workers are by no means identical. Only under the principles of communism does such a conflict of regional interest emerge with explicit acuteness.

Again, are we not entitled to ask, is not such a system, unless controlled by the most rigid dictatorial methods, continually in danger of dissolution into antagonistic regional units ? Is it workable on democratic lines on an international scale ?

[1] See Dobb, *Russian Economic Development*, pp. 409 *seq.*

CH. VIII   INTERNATIONAL COMMUNISM   219

8. This leads us to our final question. Is such a system in general compatible with the retention of democracy ?

Hitherto democracy has proved possible only when the issues to be decided were comparatively few and simple. All round us in our own day, when governments have assumed more extensive functions of control and regulation, we hear complaints of the inadequacy of the democratic machinery effectively to discharge such functions. But communism, especially communism on an international scale, involves many most complex issues. If our analysis is correct, it does not seem possible to decentralize adequately and yet keep the essentials of the system. To obviate the difficulties regarding the distribution of capital and labour which we have been examining, some mechanism of authoritative control seems essential. Is it not probable, therefore, that, under such a system, decision with regard to these issues would tend to gravitate more and more into the hands of men not subject to democratic control, and that the essence of such a government, whatever its referenda and its façade of electoral machinery, would be dictatorial ? Is it not likely that mass propaganda, stunt trials and secret coercion would become the normal instruments of government, and that, in the effort to work the vast machinery which the nature of the system necessitates, even what little at present exists of individual freedom and variety would suffer a final extinction?

International communism aims at more wealth and more freedom for all. But the means it proposes may involve the frustration of just these ends.

Lilies that fester smell far worse than weeds.

CHAPTER IX

INTERNATIONAL LIBERALISM

1. IF our analysis thus far has been correct, its results must be admitted to be profoundly disturbing. Planning on national lines leads to waste and insecurity. The international planning of particular lines of trade and industry does not remedy matters. And now there seems reason to doubt the practicability of a comprehensive planning from the centre which does not destroy just that which it was intended to preserve.

Is there no way out of this *impasse* ?

2. Let us remind ourselves of the essentials of any solution which will meet the criteria which we have laid down already.

Here on the one side are the hundreds of millions of consumers who constitute the population of the planet. On the other side are the self-same people with their various aptitudes and opportunities as producers and the mechanical and natural resources which are available. What are the essentials of an organization which shall bring it about that these productive powers are used in such a way as to satisfy as fully as possible the various wants of the citizens ?

Clearly two things are necessary. Firstly, we need an apparatus which will register the strength of demand and the relative capacity of the different instruments of production to satisfy it. Secondly, we need institutions of decentralized initiative operating in such a way as to involve a continuous tendency to apply productive resources at the point of highest return. We need to know the demands of the consumers and the relative effectiveness of different ways of satisfying them : and we need an organization of production which will bring it about that no resources can be devoted to produce any but the highest return without loss falling on those responsible for controlling them.

In the light of our earlier investigations it should not need much argument to demonstrate that the essentials of such an organization are provided by the free market and the institution of private property. A free market prices both products and the factors of production which produce them. It rewards, with higher gains, transfers to lines of production where production is more urgently needed. It punishes, with loss and reduction of income, continuance of production when the factors of production involved can produce a higher return elsewhere. The institutions of private property provide for decentralized initiative : and this initiative in turn creates the market as an organizing principle. Given their power to demand, which springs from the past value of their services and their property, the citizens exercise through the market continuous control over the future disposal of their work and their resources. The citizen, as producer, is not compelled by physical or legal coercion to put his services and his property to the uses in which they produce most in value terms. But if he chooses to refrain from doing so, his own power to consume in the future is curtailed to the extent of his refusal. As consumer the citizen buys in the cheapest market. As producer he sells in the dearest. In this way the maximum division of labour which is compatible with given tastes and given technique is continuously enforced. In this way the inhabitants of the most diverse parts, as producers, whatever the width of the jurisdiction of the government under which they happen to reside, co-operate in an organization which is tending continually to make their range of effective choice, as consumers, as wide as is compatible with an absence of arbitrary curtailment in their favour of the range of choice of their fellows.

3. But is this not the very negation of planning—a " planless economy ", an " individualistic chaos " ?

This view is widely prevalent nowadays. And,

of course, if the term planning is *by definition* to be restricted to the operations of a centralized control, then the institutions of international liberalism are indeed excluded. The principle of international liberalism is decentralization and control by the market. If we say that the term plan must not be applied to an organization in which free initiative is guided to the service of free choice by an impersonal mechanism, then we have settled a point of terminology. But we have not judged the significance of the organization.

But the terminology is surely unfortunate. The essence of a plan is that it is an attempt to shape means to ends. In a world of change the essence of a successful plan of productive organization is that it should bring about continual adaptation to changing technical conditions and changing demands of consumers. Now the various plans which we have examined hitherto do not do this. They involve a paralysis of the mechanism of adaptation: they tend to make the plan the end and the frustration of the consumers the means. They involve a tendency to a curtailment of productivity in a world which is certainly not overburdened with plenty. Surely it is wise to attempt to avoid this kind of plan, to attempt to erect a world order which is capable of adaptation and which provides incentives to adaptation. It is this which is the object of international liberalism. It is an institutional pattern especially designed to meet the difficulties of economic organization on an international scale. If planning is an attempt to create institutions conducive to the satisfaction of the citizens, then international liberalism is a plan.

It is a plan, too, in the sense that it is to be the creation of government.

It is often held that liberalism denies all functions to government. The naïve belief that unguided self-interest is necessarily conducive to public benefit is thought to be the foundation of the liberal social philosophy: and a system which is held to rest upon such a superstition is, not unnaturally, condemned without examination.

For this belief the liberals of the past are not altogether blameless. It is, of course, a grotesque libel to suggest that men such as Hume, Adam Smith or Bentham regarded government as superfluous.[1] To attribute to the great utilitarian philosophers the *jejune* presuppositions of an

[1] Mr. Keynes' celebrated pamphlet *The End of Laissez-Faire* has been regarded, both by its author and by the general public, as a great advance on the classical economists: indeed a final (or ought we to say *penultimate* ?) emancipation from the tyranny of their ideas. The full extent of our debt to Mr. Keynes is perhaps best to be estimated by a textual comparison of his own description of the *agenda* of the state and that of Adam Smith which was the basis of the classical outlook.

Let us put enlightenment first. " The most important *agenda* of the state relate not to those activities which private individuals are already fulfilling, but to those functions which fall outside the sphere of the individual, to those decisions which are made by *no one* if the state does not make them. The important thing for government to

anarchistic philosophy of society can only be regarded as propagandist rhetoric. But it may be true that, in their preoccupation with the discovery of the laws of the market, they were apt sometimes to take the market itself for granted. It may be true too that, in their zeal to expose the results of interference with the disposal of property, they may have laid insufficient emphasis upon the framework of law and order which made the institution of property possible. In this way they, and still more the politicians who simplified their analysis for popular consumption, laid themselves open to misunderstanding and misrepresentation.

But, notwithstanding all that has been said to the contrary, it is a gross misconception to suppose that government and governmental bodies do not play a most important and indispensable rôle in the liberal plan of co-operation. To emphasize this is not to claim any additional virtue for the plan. In spite of certain contemporary habits of speech, there is no intrinsic virtue either in

do is not to do things which individuals are doing already, and to do them a little better or a little worse: but to do those things which at present are not done at all " (Keynes, *The End of Laissez-Faire*, pp. 46-47).

And now for the classical night. " The sovereign has . . . thirdly, the duty of erecting and maintaining certain public works and certain public institutions which it never can be for the interest of any individual or small group of individuals, to erect and maintain: because the profit could never repay the expense to any individual or small number of individuals, though it may frequently do much more than repay it to a great society " (Adam Smith, *The Wealth of Nations* (Cannan's Edition), vol. ii, pp. 184-185).

From what a quagmire have we been delivered.

INTERNATIONAL LIBERALISM

government or the absence of government : the utilitarian calculus weighs governmental and nongovernmental actions indifferently. It is only to draw attention to an aspect of the plan, failure to understand which may lead to total misconception of the whole system. The characteristic institutions of a liberal society are inconceivable without government.

It should be obvious that they are inconceivable without security. If there is no authority armed with coercive power, the plans of the different citizens must be to some extent self-frustrating. They must provide for an apparatus of defence. This is necessarily wasteful; and it is often itself provocative. They must be short-run plans : it is not worth while planning for a long run of great uncertainty. Even so they are liable to continual disturbance. There can be no world-wide division of labour, no extensive accumulation, no elaborate organization of production if arbitrary force is not restrained by force which is stronger but which is not arbitrary.

But this is not enough. The mere absence of violence is not a sufficient condition for the efficient working of free enterprise. For co-operation to be effective it must be restrained within suitable limits by a framework of institutions. Neither property nor contract are in any sense natural. They are essentially the creation of law; and they are not simple creations. For purposes of exposition, we may sometimes speak as if property rights and the system of contract were homogeneous and simple. But if we allow ourselves to be led into supposing that this is anything but the crudest of simplifications we fall into gross error. The system of legal rights in any existing society is a matter of the utmost complexity, the actual result of centuries of legislation and judicial decision. To determine wherein these rights are to consist if they are to be conducive to the satisfaction of the public choice, to delimit their scope and their content, is a task of the utmost difficulty. In what objects are property rights to be recognized? Are they to cover ideas and inventions? Or are they to be limited to scarce material resources and their utilization? If so, what type of utilization? May a man use his property in ways which mean damage to others? If not, how is damage to be defined? Are contracts to restrict trade permissible? If so, in what circumstances? If not, what is the definition of restriction? It is in the solution of questions of this sort that the task of legal planning consists. It is in the reference of particular cases to such a system of norms that the plans thus made are continually translated into practice. The system of rights and duties of the ideal liberal society may be thought to be a good plan or it may be thought to be a bad plan. But to describe it as no plan is not to understand

CH. IX   INTERNATIONAL LIBERALISM   229

it at all. The idea of a co-ordination of human activities by means of a system of impersonal rules, within which what spontaneous relations arise are conducive to mutual benefit, is a conception, at least as subtle, at least as ambitious, as the conception of prescribing positively each action or each type of action by a central planning authority: and it is perhaps not less in harmony with the requirements of a spiritually sound society. We may blame the enthusiasts who, in their interest in what happens in the market, have paid too little attention to its necessary framework. But what shall we say of those who argue perpetually as if this framework did not exist.[1]

[1] It would be out of place in this context to elaborate the details of a desirable framework. The main preoccupation of this work is with the broadest outline of different types of plan considered in their international aspects. But it is perhaps permissible to say here that, in the opinion of the author, it is in the discovery of improvements in the admittedly defective framework of the present that one of the most important paths of future reform consists. It is not *certain* that on every possible occasion the mechanism of markets will function satisfactorily. But experience suggests that in most cases where it does not investigation shows that there is some deficiency in the law. These deficiencies are often apparently trifling. To discover them is a dull matter involving hard work and little emotional satisfaction. But it is difficult to exaggerate the practical significance of such studies. It is only necessary to compare the radically different evolution of industrial structure in England and in Germany to realize how important apparently unimportant differences in the law may be. It may be suggested that if half the energy which has been put into discovering ways in which the monopolistic activities of private enterprise may be superseded by the monopolistic activities of government organs had been devoted to discovering ways of preventing private enterprise acquiring legalized monopolistic power, the so-called monopoly problem would have ceased to be very important.

But this is not all. The provision of security and a suitable legal system is a function more important and more complex than is often suspected. But it does not exhaust the province of government. The market apparatus has its limits: and outside these limits arise certain generally acknowledged wants which, if they are not satisfied by governmental action, will either not be satisfied at all or, at best, will be satisfied very inadequately.

It is not possible or desirable exhaustively to enumerate such cases. But it is not difficult to describe their general nature. On the one hand, there exist wants which must be satisfied collectively or not satisfied at all. Of this class provision against infectious diseases is a conspicuous instance. It is comparatively useless for the individual to make private provision here. He may be willing to pay all that is technically necessary. But unless all others are doing likewise his expenditure may be ineffective. On the other hand, there arise wants which can be formulated individually, but for whose supply spontaneous contracts between private property owners is not effective. Of this class the demand for certain means of communication is typical. It is possible for individuals to offer money for means of access to different places. But, in many cases, in the absence of government action in some shape or form the supply will not be forthcoming. It is not inconceivable that an extensive road system should be satisfactorily created by private enterprise. But it is not probable: and, if it is not, then there may be need for another kind of plan.

This necessity has long been recognized. Adam Smith made it the third of his list of duties of the sovereign " to erect and maintain certain public works and certain public institutions which it can never be to the interest of any individual or small group of individuals to maintain." [1] But in recent years it has become more important. The development of technique has brought it about that many services of obvious utility are best rendered by methods which involve the use of a network of long strips of land difficult to establish save by compulsory acquisition — rail transport and canals, drainage, water supply, electricity, telegraphic and telephonic communication, and so on. It is not certain that the supply of these services is best organized on the basis of governmental or quasi-governmental monopoly. Current discussion of the matter is usually interested or superficial: the task of independent scrutiny of the most suitable institutions here has scarcely yet begun. But it is certain that, in some form or other, governmental

---

[1] See above, footnote, p. 226. An excellent short discussion of the functions of governments in this respect is to be found in Cannan, *Wealth*, chap. iv.

action is necessary. It is certain, too, that the field of such necessary action is extensive.

4. If this reasoning is correct, it is therefore wrong to regard the proposals of international liberalism as involving no plan. On the contrary, they constitute the one plan we have so far examined which does not at once display conspicuous internal weakness when conceived on a world scale.

It would be equally wrong to regard them as a plan which has ever yet been realized. Much of the order which exists even at the present owes its origin to private enterprise and the market. If there were no markets and no private enterprise our position would be even worse than it is. It is indeed one of the strongest recommendations of liberal institutions that their vitality as organizing influences is displayed even on the smallest scale and in the most adverse circumstances. But, as our earlier investigations have shown, the world today is not predominantly liberal. It is nationalist and interventionist; and the continual succession of political and economic catastrophes which this involves gives what market mechanism exists a task which no mechanism can perform. It is not liberal institutions but the absence of such institutions which is responsible for the chaos of today.

Indeed, if we preserve a sense of perspective,

the conspicuous fact that emerges from any historical survey is radically different from what the reactionaries — both fascist and communist — endeavour to make us believe. International liberalism is not a plan that has been tried and failed. It is a plan that has never yet had a full chance. The chaos of today is not something new. It is a relapse to what hitherto has been the normal condition of the human race. The difference between the economic organization of today and the economic organization of the past is great. But it is a difference of scale and technical process and potentialities for worldwide disaster. The principles have been the same. They have been sectional, monopolist, restrictionist. The results too have been similar. There has been poverty and insecurity. There was little freedom of enterprise before the nineteenth century. There were close corporations, state monopolies, restrictions on movement, sectional trade agreements, prohibitions, tariffs. . . . Only in the middle of the eighteenth century did men begin even to conceive of a world in which privilege to restrict should be restricted and in which the disposition of resources should obey, not the demands of producers for monopoly, but the demands of consumers for wealth.

For a short time it seemed as if this dream might be realized. When Adam Smith wrote *The Wealth of Nations* it seemed to him that to expect the establishment of complete freedom of trade in Great Britain was " as absurd as to expect that an Oceana or Utopia should ever be established in it ".[1] But the power of ideas, operating in a *milieu* of favourable political accidents, was stronger than even he suspected. In thirty years he had made converts of the great majority of educated Englishmen. By the middle of the nineteenth century, the Corn Laws had been repealed, restrictions on movement abolished and what to all intents and purposes were the beginnings of a liberal economic system established in Great Britain.

The influence of these changes was not confined to Great Britain. The internal policy of the United States of America, although lacking much in power to control the excesses of the frontier spirit, was predominantly liberal. And for a brief period indeed it seemed as if the countries of the European mainland would develop similar institutions. From the forties to the seventies of the nineteenth century the trend of legislation almost everywhere was liberal. Tariffs were lowered. Personal unfreedom was abolished. Enterprise was freed. Monopolies were dissolved. International division of labour was extended. And the consequential increase of wealth was spectacular.

But reaction was not long in asserting itself.

---

[1] *Wealth of Nations* (Cannan's Edition), p. 435.

From the seventies onwards the tide began to flow in the opposite direction. In Central and Eastern Europe the ideas of international liberalism had never taken firm root. The idea that production could be organized without the existence of an organizer who gave orders, as Frederick William gave orders to his guards, was not easily assimilated by minds few of which had ever really thrown off the habits of intellectual sycophancy of autocratic courts. The failure of the '48 and the unification of Germany by Blood and Iron created an atmosphere in which the principles of mercantilism were once more respectable. The Physiocrats were condemned: the Cameralists exalted. The systems of List and Schmoller took the place of the system of Smith and Ricardo. Neither the socialists on the left nor the conservatives on the right, each only the representatives of special interests, ever grasped the view that co-operation without regulation from the centre could be anything other than chaos. The reimposition of the iron and steel duties by Bismarck at the end of the seventies, and his explicit adoption of the principles of imperialism, were the death-knell of liberalism in Germany. The practice of the totalitarian Third Reich is only the practice of Bismarckian Germany writ large.

There were other influences tending in the same direction. In its origins socialism, equally with liberalism, was rationalist and utilitarian. It rested on the belief, clearly susceptible of reasonable discussion, that there was a technique of economic organization superior to a system of free enterprise. But early efforts to demonstrate this were not successful; and the attempt was soon abandoned. With the decline of the French Utopians, socialism relapsed into the messianic mysticism of Marxian determinism; or it allied itself with the special interests of trade-union restrictionism. Its propaganda, although professedly international, had the effect of weakening belief in the free market and strengthening the movement for the revival of national controls. It thus played directly into the hands of the reaction. The nationalist reactionaries well knew how to steal the thunder of the socialists and present it in a " more human ", " more practicable " form.

Nor must the mistakes of the liberal reformers be left out of the picture here. There is no doubt that the early liberals had not thought out completely the implications of their position. They were weak on the problem of associations, and they did not really grasp the problem of national sovereignties. In consequence, they sometimes followed policies which created new opportunities for privilege and emphasized national differences : and at every step the representatives of special interests were alert to exploit their blunders. The dictatorship of the consumer is a drastic purge of inefficiency : and those sections of the community whose privileges were menaced were not over-scrupulous about their methods of defence.

But when all this is taken into account, it is the nationalist reaction which must claim the main credit for arresting the liberal revolution. The claim of Hitler to have saved Europe from Marx and Lenin may be dubious. But Bismarck certainly "saved" us from Cobden and Adam Smith. In the history of the last sixty years it is the influence of German thought and German policy which has been dominant. The existence, at the centre of European civilization, of a Power whose statesmen and thinkers openly rejected liberalism and regarded the atavistic ideals of imperialism as the be-all and end-all of policy, exercised an influence which it is difficult to exaggerate. It gave the tone to thought and legislation even in countries where liberalism persisted. British imperialism was made in Germany, and the paternalism of the official liberal party in Great Britain was modelled on Bismarck's "Social State". It dominated foreign policy. It accentuated national divisions and international alliances. And in the end it brought about the Great War in which liberal institutions began to founder and in whose aftermath they have been nearly swept away.

·International liberalism is not a plan which has been tried and failed. It is a plan which has never been carried through — a revolution crushed by reaction ere it had time to be fully tested.

5. We can see this all the more vividly if we try to sketch out for ourselves some of the changes which are necessary to make international liberalism a reality. To imagine that, in the present state of opinion, these changes will come about may be as absurd as to imagine the establishment of an Oceana or a Utopia. But it is always useful to know the significance of different directions of movement. And if we have found that other plans lead to institutions which seem to be ultimately unworkable, it is, at least, interesting to know whether this plan would be doomed to frustration for similar reasons.

We do not have to look far before coming to the main requirement. According to the outline of the functions of government which we have already made, the first essential is security. There cannot be an orderly international division of labour, there cannot exist the complicated network of financial and economic relations essential to the proper development of the earth's resources, if the citizens are continually in danger of violence. In the present state of technique as regards communications and production, this is more important than it ever has been. Without order, no economy : without peace, no welfare.

But it is in just this most elementary requirement of a comprehensive international plan that our present organization is most conspicuously lacking. There is world economy. But there is no world polity. The different national states each arm against the other. Between their members there is not the ordered freedom of the liberal state but the brutish anarchy of the state of nature. The opportunities of division of labour make us members one of another. But for lack of proper governmental machinery we make war or prepare for war continually. We should regard it as absurd if the inhabitants of the county of London maintained armed forces for defence against the inhabitants of the surrounding counties and the inhabitants of surrounding counties maintained armed forces against them. We should regard it as childish, atavistic, wasteful, if not actually productive of chaos. Yet, because of the division of the world into national units, similar arrangements between areas, equally interdependent and equally indistinguishable by any criteria other than the arbitrary heritage of past governmental arrangements, are not merely taken for granted as inevitable but even regarded as contributing to the general good. These are no doubt matters of ultimate valuation. Whether it is a good thing or a bad thing to kill without judicial process is a question which, even at the present day, is often decided differently according to the nationality of the victims. But this thing is certain. The nationalistic anarchy is wasteful. Whatever value we may put on the military virtues as such, there can be no doubt that, at the present time, the existence of this apparatus for eliciting such virtues is more costly, in terms of the other things we have to sacrifice, than any other luxury the human race affords. How much misery might have been avoided, how much poverty prevented, had the accident of history not divided the seat of sovereignty.

It is just here that we can perceive one of the main deficiencies of nineteenth-century liberalism. It was the great achievement of the men of those days to have realized the harmony of interest of the inhabitants of different national areas. But they did not sufficiently realize that the achievement of this harmony was only possible within a framework of international security. They thought that if they demonstrated the wastefulness and futility of economic and political warfare it was enough. If each national state were limited to the performance of the functions proper to a liberal government there would be no occasion for international conflict. There would be no need for a super-national authority.

But this was a grave error. The harmony of interests which they perceived to be established by the institutions of property and the market

CH. IX INTERNATIONAL LIBERALISM 241

necessitated, as they had demonstrated, an apparatus for maintaining law and order. But whereas *within* national areas such an apparatus, however imperfect, existed, *between* national areas there was no apparatus at all. Within the national areas they relied upon the coercive power of the state to provide the restraints which harmonized the interests of the different individuals. Between the areas they relied only upon demonstration of common interest and the futility of violence: their outlook here, that is to say, was implicitly not liberal but anarchist. But the anarchist position is untenable. It is true that, for the citizen who does not love war as such, abstention from violence is an obvious matter of self-interest. It is true that, in the long run, aggression seldom pays the aggressor, and that even victory is associated with impoverishment. But if we are not content to rely on such arguments for the preservation of order within the nation, we have no reason to believe that such reliance would be effective in preserving international order.

> Es kann der Beste nicht in Frieden leben
> Wenn es dem bösen Nachtbar nicht gefällt.

The existence of *one* state whose leaders have evil intentions can frustrate the co-operation of a world of peaceful peoples. It is not by the demonstration that burglary and gangsterdom do not pay that we restrain the activities of burglars and gangsters : it is by the maintenance of a mechanism of restraint. And it will not be without a mechanism of restraint that international burglary and gangsterdom are banished from the face of the earth.[1]

" A man must be far gone in Utopian speculations who can seriously doubt that if . . . states . . . be wholly disunited or only united in partial confederacies, the subdivisions into which they might be thrown would have frequent and violent contests with each other. To presume a want of motive for such contests as an argument against their existence would be to forget that men are ambitious, vindictive and rapacious. To look for a continuation of harmony between a number of independent, unconnected sovereignties in the same neighbourhood would be to disregard the uniform course of human events, and to set at defiance the accumulated experience of ages." [2]

But how is the apparatus of restraint to be provided ?

It is becoming very obvious that mere associations of sovereign states are ineffective. The confederation—the *Staatenbund*—has never been

---

[1] This is a subject which Cannan made his own long before it was a matter of popular discussion. See especially his valedictory address to the London School of Economics, " Adam Smith as an Economist ": *An Economist's Protest*, p. 417 *seq.* Also a lecture on " International Anarchy from the Economic Point of View ", reprinted in the same place, p. 65 *seq.*

[2] Hamilton, *The Federalist* (Everyman Edition), p. 20.

very successful: and in our own day its weaknesses are only too painfully evident. So long as the different states retain their sovereignty, so long can decrees against them be enforced ultimately only by armed alliances of other states. Every word that was written by the founders of the American constitution against the confederal form of government has been vindicated again in our own time by the history of the League of Nations.

"Government", wrote Hamilton, "implies the power of making laws. It is essential to the idea of law that it be attended with a sanction. ... If there be no penalty attached to disobedience, the resolutions or commands which pretend to be laws will, in fact, amount to nothing more than advice or recommendation. This penalty, whatever it may be, can only be inflicted in two ways: by the agency of the courts and ministers of justice, or by military force: by the COERCION of the magistracy, or by the COERCION of arms. The first kind can evidently apply only to men: the last kind must of necessity be employed against bodies politic or communities or states. It is evident that there is no process of a court by which the observance of the laws can in the last resort be enforced. Sentences may be denounced against them for violations of their duty: but these sentences can only be carried into execution by the sword. . . .

"In every political association which is formed upon the principle of uniting in a common interest a number of lesser sovereignties, there will be found a kind of eccentric tendency in the subordinate or inferior ones by the operation of which there will be a perpetual effort in each to fly off from the common centre. . . ." [1]

Only the surrender of sovereignty, of the right to make war, by the national governments can remove the danger.

But a completely unitary world state is neither workable nor desirable. Its unworkability depends essentially upon the extent of the area and the complexity of the language conditions over which it would have jurisdiction. We have seen this difficulty in surveying the possibilities of international communism. It would arise even in a completely liberal system. For a central authority to be responsible for roads and public health both in Austria and Australia would be absurd. Nor could we be sure that such a body would be an efficient safeguard of liberty. Caligula once wished that the whole Roman people could be united in one head so that at a single blow he might have the supreme ecstasy of decapitating it. That great Leviathan, the unitary world state, might present similar temptations to our modern sadists. If independent sovereignty is chaos, the unrestricted unitary state might be death.

[1] *Op. cit.* pp. 71-72.

There is only one solution to this stupendous problem. The first need of the world is not economic but political revolution. It is not necessary that a world state should have powers unrestricted by constitution. But it is necessary that the national states should surrender certain rights to an international authority. The right of making war and the power to do so must be given up. But they need not give up all their rights of independent government; and the rights of the international authority must also be limited. There must be neither alliance nor complete unification, but Federation; neither *Staatenbund*, nor *Einheitsstaat*, but *Bundesstaat*.

Here we once more see the far-reaching wisdom of the founders of the American constitution. They did not produce a perfect constitution. Perfection of political arrangements is not to be hoped for, is indeed not even conceivable. It is obvious that both in the American Federation which exists and in any world or smaller federation which might be modelled on it, there remain great problems of providing for proper adaptation of the division of federal and state powers and adjusting the areas of regional administration. No sane person will pretend that the American constitution today provides an instrument which is at all perfectly adapted to the necessities of government under present technical conditions.[1] But when all these obvious deficiencies are taken into account, the fact remains that they did construct an instrument which has reconciled the interests of a multitude of people over vast stretches of the earth's surface and has created an area of peace and internal freedom for economic co-operation which is without precedent in history. They did establish a principle which offers the one hope of escape from the fear of destruction which today overshadows humanity. And when we contrast the peace and the riches of that great Union with the chaos and anarchy of the unhappy nations of Europe we know that this was something worth doing, worth preserving, worth fighting to preserve. We can read Abraham Lincoln's noble dedication of the dead at Gettysburg and know that his claims were just.

6. It is not the purpose of this chapter to draw up the articles of a world federation. Our aim, here as throughout these reflections, is to suggest principles rather than to elaborate policy. But it will help to clarify our ideas if we explore a little further the functions in such a system of such bodies as now are sovereign states. We will ignore the obvious unsuitability for any kind of administrative function of many of the present national

---

[1] The implicit criticism in the propositions of the next section of this chapter should be sufficient to guard against misunderstanding here.

areas. The problem of the appropriate area for federal organization of any sort is a problem of the utmost importance, and it would be an important feature of any rational constitution that provisions were made for periodic adjustments. But for our purposes this may be disregarded. Assuming that there is not to be complete unification, we enquire what functions would be best discharged by the local " states " if the principles of international liberalism are to be realized.

It should be clear from what we have seen already in earlier chapters that there is no place for such bodies, however geographically constituted, as regulators of inter-area trade. It would be the object of a liberal world federation to create the maximum scope for international division of labour : and any restriction of trading between governmental areas would be totally alien to its intention. In so far as a liberal system involves a framework of legal regulation—and we have seen that this is of the utmost importance—the constitution should bring it about that such a framework was federal—that is to say, that the law of property and contract the world over was unified and administered on uniform principles. That the authorities of local " states " should retain the power to prevent the citizens who happened to inherit their areas from selling their produce where the demand was greatest and buying their goods where the supply was cheapest would be inimical to the international liberal plan.[1]

For the same reason, it would be inappropriate that such local authorities should have power to limit the movement of labour or capital. If the different states of the American Federation had had the right to limit migration or investment, there can be little doubt that some of them would have done so. But it would have been an illiberal system. That the people who happen to reside within a particular administrative area should have the right to prevent people elsewhere having as free access to co-operation with the owners of the fixed property within the area as they themselves have would give rise—as it does in the world of independent states today—to positions of monopoly and privilege. The owners of fixed property in the different areas are compelled, on pain of loss of potential income, to put their resources to those uses which satisfy the most urgent demands. Why should those who dispose of services which are mobile be prevented

---

[1] It should be remembered that here as elsewhere we are discussing types of planning, not tactics of planning policy. Whether it would be wise to make the surrender of fiscal power an essential of any world federation is quite a separate question. It is arguable that if the national states could be induced to surrender the powers of making peace or war, this would be enough as a beginning : and nothing that is said in this chapter or elsewhere should be construed as attempting to decide this question in advance. As is emphasized continually, the object of the essay is to contrast alternatives, not to formulate policy. It is obvious that to plan the " deplanning " of the interventionism of the last half-century would demand a treatise in itself.

from doing likewise ? It is sometimes urged that there are "social" arguments, whatever that may mean, against complete freedom of migration. Most of these are based upon reasoning so obviously fragile or so fundamentally intolerant as to be scarcely worth discussion.[1] But whatever their validity, it is surely certain that, if it were necessary to impose limitations on the movement of any class of citizens, or on the movement of their capital, that would be a function which should only be performed by the federal authority, never by the local states.

But what, then, should be the power of the different local authorities ?

[1] The one argument against perfectly free migration which is likely to be interesting to international liberals is that elaborated by Cannan (*Wealth*, 3rd Edition, p. 287) concerning differential fertility. *If* any people shows a chronic incapacity to restrain their multiplication, whatever their economic circumstances, then Cannan argued, " it is probably desirable that it should be confined within as narrow limits as possible. It is better that it should learn that over-population is an evil, and how to avoid it, in one country or continent, than after extending it all over the world." Analytically, accepting the utilitarian criteria of policy, the argument is surely valid. But its applicability depends on the assumption that such peoples actually exist. In present conditions it seems as if birth control were likely to become universal. Mr. Carr Saunders suggests that it may even be widely adopted in India (Carr Saunders, *World Population*, p. 277). And it has yet to be shown that, where immigrants from high-birth-rate countries settle in low-birth-rate areas, they do not rapidly—some would say, too rapidly—assimilate their habits in this respect to those of their new neighbours. This obviously is a matter about which wide generalization would be foolish. But if it could be shown that there are people whose habits will never be other than conformable to the generalizations of the first edition of the *Essay on Population*, it is still clear, as argued above, that the regulation of their movements is a matter for a world, rather than a local, authority. Local authorities have much too strong a temptation to use this as a pretext for local monopoly.

It is a significant comment on the degree to which the ideals of international liberalism have yet spread that, in the vast literature which has been devoted both to the economic functions of "*the*" state and to the problems of international government and international economic relations, scarcely any attention is devoted to this fundamentally important subject. In the literature of public finance, there is some discussion of problems of double taxation and the relationship between rates and taxes. But of the positive functions of state and local government activity and expenditure there is hardly anything which, from the point of view of the international economist, is at all interesting or illuminating. The theory of the functions of local government is discussed almost always in terms of the interests of the inhabitants of the locality, rather than in terms of the common interest. The theory of the functions of "*the*" state is discussed without any regard whatever to the relations between states and the general world interest.

Fortunately there is one exception. One of the main preoccupations which dominated the work of Edwin Cannan was precisely this question of the way in which the activities of separate governmental authorities, operating within a larger community, could be so directed as to tend to the common interest: and, after much seeking, he arrived at what is certainly the most plausible solution which has yet been put forward. Unfortunately, with characteristic modesty, he developed his views in a context of such specialized application—the last chapter of a very technical work on the history of local rates in England—that it is doubtful whether, even among professional economists, any but his own pupils have ever been really aware of them.[1]

Broadly speaking, the principle is as follows. The different local authorities, whether "national" or "local", should pursue such policies as, without restriction, should give the greatest value to the resources permanently fixed within their jurisdiction. The rationale of this maxim is probably best seen by a short account of its genesis.

It is clear, from its context, that Cannan was led to his solution by a consideration of the problems of small local government authorities. It is obvious that, so far as such authorities are concerned, it is not legitimate to assume the absence of the possibility of migration into, or out of, the area. But if this is so, he argued, then a policy chiefly directed to benefit the "inhabitants" by taxing resources which could not leave the neighbourhood was bound to lead to an arbitrary distribution of population. The inhabitants are merely the people who happen to find it worth

[1] The history of his different attempts to discover a solution is recorded in the preface to his *Economic Outlook*, pp. 31-35.

while to live in the neighbourhood for the time being. To tax the fixed resources in the interests of such a body rather than in the interests of the world at large, would simply mean that immigration would be encouraged without permanent benefit to the immigrants and that the rents of the fixed resources would be dissipated in ways which would definitely encourage maldistribution of effort. But if, instead of this, the local authority regarded itself chiefly as the custodian of the fixed resources within its area, and if it did things which tended to raise the value of those resources but which, because of technical difficulties of arranging spontaneous co-operation, were not done or were done imperfectly by their owners, then it would be acting in harmony with the general requirement of the liberal system that resources should so be used as to secure maximum value in price terms. We have seen already that there are many services for which there is obvious need but for which, because of the difficulty of individual pricing or because of the difficulty of securing spontaneous co-operation between the owners of different pieces of the earth's surface, the system of private enterprise does not always make provision. The provision of roads, trunk sewers, lighting, water supply, parks, are obvious examples. It was in the facilitating and the provision of such arrangements that Cannan conceived the most essential duty of local authorities to consist.

INTERNATIONAL LIBERALISM

But this principle, as he went on to urge, applies not merely to counties but to countries: or, more accurately, to larger as to smaller area jurisdiction. There are some functions of this sort, the provision of lighting for instance, which can perhaps best be arranged or supervised by the smallest local government authority. There are others, such as the provision of arterial roads or the preservation as parks of large stretches of countryside, which demand the activities of different national authorities or even groups of such authorities. Others, the provision of water for instance, probably involve the jurisdiction of areas of intermediate size. And the co-ordination of such activities where they overlap again involves a hierarchy of decentralized governmental bodies. With changing technique the extent of the area most appropriate to initiate or to control such activities varies. It is one of the permanent difficulties of national as of international government, while providing for decentralized initiative, to maintain adequate flexibility of regional administration. Since the private property system cannot fully operate here, some substitute for the influence of loss and bankruptcy has to be devised. And this is not easy. If it were only because of the magnitude of the problems which are thus involved, it would be desirable that the governmental bodies which must necessarily deal with them should be relieved as far as possible from other preoccupations. But whatever the difficulties of detail, the fundamental principle is clear. The local authorities, whether national or municipal, should have the maximum freedom to develop, without restriction of trade, investment or migration, the value of the fixed resources which are best dealt with by their jurisdiction.

There are, however, other governmental functions which do not fall under this heading, but which in fact would probably be discharged by local authorities. The relief of destitution and some instruction of the young are functions which presumably would be discharged by public authority within most liberal systems. The relief of destitution, by definition, is not a function which can be evoked by the profit incentive: and the incompatibility of contracts with infants with the principles of personal liberty precludes exclusive reliance on the price and property mechanism in regard to education. Because the price mechanism is inapplicable in these cases there are great difficulties in arranging principles of distribution which do not weaken individual initiative and family responsibility. But, in some form or other, they are functions which have to be discharged.

Now it should be very clear from what has been said already that they are not functions which can be discharged by small local authorities without grave danger. For small local government authorities to be responsible for the discharge of such functions is to invite maldistribution of population and administrative chaos. Experience in Great Britain and in the United States shows the grave disadvantages in local, or even in state, relief of any kind of destitution. Indeed we may lay it down as a general principle that, whereas when it is a matter of improving by governmental action the value of fixed resources (that is, of supplementing the principle of private property) the smaller the area of administration the better, when it is a matter of organizing what may be called communistic relief (that is, of supplementing the principle of family responsibility) the contrary principle applies. The wider the area of administration, the more equitable the burden of taxation, the more economical the distribution of resources.

Nevertheless wide administrative units have their limits. Local habits and conditions differ widely in different parts, and long before the unit of administration and initiative had become coterminous with the area of a world federation it would become impossibly unwieldy. For good or for bad, it would be inevitable that a large measure of initiative should be left to authorities smaller than the federal power.

If this is done, however, the danger we have already recognized arises. Unless the different authorities keep more or less in step, there is the possibility that their policies may give rise to undesirable movements both of capital and of labour—of capital to escape taxation, of labour to receive benefits. This danger is inevitable. And it is not overcome completely by larger units of administration. But, in a system whose constitution involved the fundamental rights of freedom of movement and investment, it is probable that the danger would itself be a safeguard. So long as migration and investment were free, and were kept free by the fundamental constitution, it is not likely that the authorities of the different areas would break step for long without experiencing considerable difficulty. The big problems of migration and the social services have arisen in the past, not because of the existence of social services as such, but because under the political constitution, under independent state or municipal authority, these services were permitted to carry with them laws of settlement, limitations of migration and investment. If freedom to migrate and freedom to invest are preserved, the danger of maldistribution of resources from the existence of decentralized administration of communistic governmental functions, although it still exists, is greatly diminished.

This suggests one further point which it is perhaps useful to mention explicitly. It is the burden of the preceding analysis that, in a liberal system, the provision of all those things which can be provided by private enterprise should be left to private enterprise. Governmental bodies, whatever their size, have quite enough to do without competing with private business. Nevertheless, it would be ill-advised to make it a fundamental feature of any world constitution that governments should never embark on this kind of business. The arguments may be all against their actually doing so. But it is not inconceivable that in some cases it might be desirable. The important thing is, not that governments should never engage in business, but that, if they do, they should not be empowered to prevent private enterprise from competing with them, and that they should be subject to the same rules of fair competition as the others. What is essential is, not that there should be no government *enterprise*, but that there should be no government *monopoly*. If government enterprise can satisfy demand better than private enterprise according to the test of a market which is not rigged by governmental regulations or subsidies in favour of itself, the liberal utilitarian criterion is satisfied. It is clear that this is a condition which has seldom, if ever, yet been realized.[1]

[1] How many British socialists, for instance, would be willing to make the experiment of nationalizing, not all the mines in the country, but one or two suitably chosen mines, and operating them without subsidy in competition with the others ? This is really an acid test

7. We have now sketched the outlines of the chief principles of international liberal planning. There must be security. There must be a legal framework appropriate to the effective working of the system of markets and private property. In various ways, some of which we have endeavoured to indicate, government machinery must provide supplements to the principles of private property and family responsibility. The citizens, as consumers, distribute their incomes between the different commodities according to their private preferences for themselves or for others. As producers, they sell their services and the use of their property in ways which they hope will bring the highest return compatible with their desire for security and private amenity. They are thus led, by the artificial institution of the market, into lines of production which serve their preferences as consumers.

Before concluding it will be instructive to take one more general survey and, assuming such a plan to be put into operation and assuming a will to maintain its essential features, to ask how it might be expected actually to work. We defer, until the concluding chapter, consideration of the political obstacles which at present prevent its establishment.

_{whether the intention of nationalization is monopolistic gain or technical efficiency. There is no reason to suppose that the technical optimum in this industry is very large.}

If the argument of this chapter is correct, it would appear that the plan would be free from large internal contradictions. It would not suffer from those great difficulties of principle from which the other plans we have examined have all appeared to suffer. Under liberalism the machinery works one way. It is not attempted to do one thing with one part and something logically incompatible with that with another. Moreover, it has the advantage that it can be achieved by stages. The socialist plan is all or nothing; for, as we have seen, national socialism leads not towards but away from international socialism. But if the world will not accept complete international liberalism all at once, it still remains true that the more liberalism it introduces into its arrangements the greater will be the resulting gain of wealth and stability. A single country or group of countries can pursue many of the aims of international liberalism in a world given over otherwise to interventionism and central planning and enjoy some at least of its benefits.

But it is important to make clear the limitations of such a system. The analysis of earlier chapters should have shown that many current criticisms are based on misapprehension. It is not planless. It is not chaotic. It is not responsible for international political frictions. But we only weaken the strong case which can be made out for it as the most practicable scheme which has yet been devised for a necessarily imperfect society if we do not explicitly recognize the respects in which it is open to criticism.

It should be recognized, in the first place, that the disposition of resources actually achieved, even under the most favourable conditions conceivable, will not be minutely optimal as in the abstractions of mathematical economics. At any moment, if only because of the continual development of new wants and new techniques, some producers will be found in a quasi-monopolistic position. It is wrong to claim, for a liberal system, continuous achievement of the perfect competitive equilibrium of pure theory. Indeed it is probable that some of the current strictures on such a system arise from excessive preoccupation with these abstractions, to the neglect of investigation of the way in which institutions which limit competition will actually work in practice. What can be claimed for the system in this respect is not that it eliminates all those indivisibilities of factor combination and imperfections of the market which give rise to quasi-monopolistic positions, but rather that, if there is no statutory support for restrictive practices, and if the law is properly framed, any attempt to exploit these positions, outside very narrow margins, will be frustrated by new competition. The wider the market and the freer the

INTERNATIONAL LIBERALISM

range of choice, the smaller will these imperfections be.

In the second place, it should be recognized that the system would not be free from error. Production takes place in anticipation of demand. The extent to which demand is actually satisfied depends upon the extent to which the anticipations of the producers have been correct. It is not claimed that isolated producers would not make mistakes. No system is superior to the people who work it. It is claimed only that if they do make mistakes, then the market imposes penalties which compel a revision of their plans. It is an essential feature of the liberal system that the leaders of industry are not rescued from the consequences of their own error. The governmental bodies have their own work to do. It is no part of this work to frustrate the guiding pressures of the market.

Nor is it to be claimed that collective error would be impossible. The false anticipations of particular producers may be contagious and may lead to more extensive mistakes. It is absurd to regard the catastrophic fluctuations of the post-war world, cluttered up with interventionism and international monetary instability, as a model of the probable dynamics of a system of economic freedom. It is a model only of the internal contradictions of a system which heightens risks, diminishes adaptability and paralyses the market without providing an efficient substitute.[1] Nevertheless it would not be reasonable to claim immunity from general fluctuations for a system freed from these elements. But it would be reasonable to claim that the more extensive fluctuations would seem to be due to, or at least conditioned by, monetary influences which it should not be impossible to diminish. We do not yet know all about these matters. But it has yet to be shown that, within the general system of the market, it is not possible to develop institutions which produce a more beneficial damping effect than anything possible outside it.[2] And it may be claimed, too, that, given the stabilizing influence of a sound monetary system, the movement of relative prices and costs provides correctives to such errors more effective than otherwise seem practicable.

Finally, we must recognize that even if these working frictions were abolished, the system would involve some inequality of income.

[1] In my *Great Depression* I have developed this thesis at length; see especially chap. iv. " The Causes of Deflation ".

[2] I hope that such a degree of generality at this point will not be thought to be disingenuous. As readers of my *Great Depression* will know, I am rather sceptical of the merits of certain current proposals for stabilization of price levels, although I do not exclude the possibility of many improvements in our present arrangements. But both the proposals I reject and the proposals I would urge fall within the framework of an essentially liberal society. Since at this point I do not wish to diverge into all the arcana of current monetary controversy, I have intentionally used here a form of words which I think would be acceptable to the majority on either side of this discussion. In Chapter X below, however, I discuss some of the international aspects of what I regard as a sound monetary system.

CH. IX INTERNATIONAL LIBERALISM

In a liberal society, the organization of production is controlled by expenditure in the market. The market produces what the consumers choose, bidding for goods according to their incomes. Now for the liberal utilitarian, it is no objection to such a system that the choices which are thus satisfied are not necessarily " good " choices, that the goods which are produced are very often, from his point of view, detestable and vulgar. The liberal does not claim that the satisfactions which result from spontaneous choice are necessarily " good " satisfactions ; he claims only that it is possible that they may be. Whereas, he would urge, satisfactions which are chosen for, and imposed upon, adult men and women cannot fall into that category. He would argue that, if we object to the preferences of our fellow citizens, we should try to persuade them to choose otherwise, not deprive them of the right of choice. It is, however, a more solid objection that the incomes out of which demand is made are unequal. That demand is free is not an objection for the liberal. But that it is unequal he must regard as a much more solid objection. He knows that there is no probability that the distribution of income will be necessarily proportionate to need. To this extent he must regard the end product of the market process as imperfect.

But it is important here to be clear as to what kind of inequality of income is involved. Much inequality of income is due to monopolistic restriction. Indeed a strong case can be made out for the view that statistically this is much the most important. In an international redistribution on equalitarian lines it would be the high incomes of the average worker of western democracies, not high property incomes, which would provide the greater part available for redistribution; and as we have seen, some, at any rate, of the difference between wages in different places is due to limitations on migration. In so far as monopolistic privileges are destroyed, this type of inequality would tend to disappear. The establishment of competitive conditions on an international scale would release vast equalizing tendencies. It is possible, too, to think of tax systems not incompatible with the fundamental liberal principle, which would diminish inequality of property holdings.[1] And, as we have seen, these govern-

[1] To avoid misunderstanding, I ought perhaps to be explicit concerning the attitude to the institution of inheritance implied in this position.

I do not regard inheritance as any more " natural " than property. It must be justified, if at all, by appeal not to natural rights but to social utility. But I do not believe that it is desirable to abolish it. The wealth of society depends in part on the volume of accumulation. If all forms of inheritance were abolished, either the property would have to be held and maintained by the state, which, for reasons which I hope have been made clear above, I do not think would be desirable; or the total volume of accumulation would be limited to the savings of one generation, which would certainly not be enough to redeem the present population of the world from gross poverty.

This view, however, does not prevent me from believing that it is possible to modify gross inequality by taxation: and I see no reason why this should necessarily lead to an important diminution of the volume of saving. I do not believe in the celebrated Rignano

mental functions which supplement the institution of the family may be conceived to go far to mitigate inequality of opportunity for personal talent. Nevertheless it is important to realize that, when all this is done, the determination of income by market value of services and the hire of private property does make some inequality inevitable. So long as the system is in a state of change and so long as different people possess different amounts of property, so long will the determination of incomes on this principle involve some inequality of power to demand.

Now this is certainly regrettable. If we could plan a system which would work as well as the system of free markets and private enterprise and would yet preserve more equality of income, it would be profoundly to be welcomed. But we have found no substitute for these institutions. And, if there is no substitute, then if we prefer

scheme, since that would either limit accumulation to the savings of two or three generations or result in progressive socialization. But I should be in favour of inheritance taxes, graduated not on the size of the estate left but on the size of the inheritance received. This would encourage the division of large estates. But it would not lead to their dissipation; and it would be free from the disadvantages of the principle of the *legitim*, which has the effect of encouraging small families. Modern liberals have been so fascinated by the Rignano scheme, which is definitely socialistic in intention, that they have tended to overlook this obvious development of the legacy duties, which is much more in harmony with the principles they profess to follow. True liberals should want more property all round, not less. There is no doubt that, although more costly to collect than the present estate duties, this type of taxation would be administratively possible. (See Appendix XXVII to the *Report of the Colwyn Committee on National Debt and Taxation*.)

wealth to poverty and international order to nationalistic chaos, we must accept this by-product of the market system as the necessary cost of these benefits. If the maintenance of efficient production depends upon the existence of the system of free enterprise, it is not correct to argue as if the incomes from property are obtained at the expense of incomes from other sources—as is indeed the case with the gains of monopolistic restriction. In a truly competitive system the incomes which arise from property ownership are not deductions from other incomes: they are additional to them. If private property were abolished, then the other incomes would be lower. The toleration of inequality is surely a small price to pay for the reduction of poverty.

But this is not all. If our argument is correct the free market and private property are conducive to the most efficient utilization of material resources. But they are conducive, too, to the preservation of liberty and culture. In the multiplicity of buyers and sellers there is security against the excesses of tied personal relationships. There is no guarantee of personal independence so secure as the institution of private property.

Here, too, it is important not to claim too much. The market is not always free. The institution of property may be the object of false valuations. The *littérateurs* of a sterile age have made us very familiar with the misfortunes of unpropertied men who fall out with bad employers : and they have not forborne to expatiate on the petty vulgarities of the rentier. But they have not devoted such minute attention to the unpleasant possibilities of other forms of society. Yet before we condemn one set of institutions, we should surely enquire concerning the alternatives. Under capitalism, despite occasional injustice, he who quarrels with his employer may hope to get on with another. And, for all the pettiness which may sometimes be bred by property or by the spectacle of property, it is incontestable that the self-same institution enables the individual to withstand the pressure of the powerful and, in defiance of popular condemnation, to create new values for humanity.[1] It is not clear that there would be this degree of liberty elsewhere. In the centrally planned society there is one employer and no property. It is not contended that there would be no spiritual values in such a state of society. Even

[1] Perhaps one example is permissible. If the painter Cézanne had not been a man of property, his pictures would never have been painted. No one who has the slightest acquaintance with the history of nineteenth-century art in France can believe that any official academy, however enlightened, would have admitted his claims to be an official artist. Even Manet thought he was a fool. Yet this is a man of whom it can be said without exaggeration that he gave new eyes to our generation, a master before whose works we have to think of the greatest masterpieces of Rembrandt and Giotto to evoke a parallel profundity of emotion. It is an odd thing, probably only to be explained on psychopathological grounds, that the lesser artists and poets of our day should have dallied so often with collectivist dreams. There is no Bohemia in the collectivist state.

the regime of the Aztecs was marked by some aesthetic achievement. But we may legitimately ask how much of what we regard as most precious in the cultural inheritance of the West would have survived the pressures of societies in which there was no private property and no free market. It is to be feared, very little.

We should not claim for liberalism that the world it could produce would be perfect. The poets and the thinkers of liberalism, the inheritors of the great classical tradition of Europe, have not shown much tendency to entertain such vain hopes. But we may claim that, with all its deficiencies, it would still provide a safeguard for happiness and spontaneity more efficient than any other which has yet been suggested.

CHAPTER X

INTERNATIONAL MONEY

1. It has not been the intention of the preceding argument to discuss in any detail particular features of the international liberal plan. The aim throughout has been to depict the plan as a whole, to outline the main principles in their proper perspective.

There is one subject, however, which it is desirable to discuss more fully, the question of the status of money. Ought money to be a "national" or a "federal" function ? Should there be different independent national currencies or should the monetary system of the world be unified ? These are questions which bring us back from the high abstractions of the last two chapters to matters much nearer to those developments of contemporary policy from which our analysis started.

In the last two chapters we have been discussing changes which, even if it were decided that they were desirable, could not be fully realized in the lifetime of men now living. But in the question of national or international money we stand at this moment on the brink of important decisions. The nineteenth century went far to evolve an international money. In the twentieth century we have gone far to destroy it. To discover whether, from the ruins of the international system of the past, we should attempt some reconstruction, or whether we should go forward with the monetary nationalism of recent years, is a matter of the utmost practical importance. It is to the discussion of this question that the present chapter is devoted.[1]

2. It will help to clear our ideas for the main investigation if we commence by tracing, in rather more detail than was attempted in Chapter II, the fundamental causes which give rise to the so-called international monetary problem.

If we were to ask an intelligent layman the fundamental cause of the breakdown of the international gold standard, he would probably reply that it was the difficulty of monetary transfer. The different centres which abandoned gold could not obtain, at rates near the gold parity, sufficient foreign exchange to meet the necessities of trans-

---

[1] This chapter is devoted to the discussion of matters which, because they deal with money and income, may seem rather more technical than the subject of other chapters. Readers who experience difficulty at this point may pass to the next chapter, where the discussion once more becomes general. But it has been attempted to keep the present discussion as free as possible from extreme technicality, and it is hoped that even the complete layman will not find the general drift of the argument very difficult to follow.

fer. They were, therefore, obliged either to resort to exchange control and planned trade, or to allow the rate of exchange to find another more possible level.

Now, we may leave undiscussed the question whether this description really applies in detail to the actual circumstances of successive crises in the different financial centres. We will not investigate whether, for instance, the United States of America was so destitute of gold at the time that the gold standard was abandoned that a really acute transfer crisis was actually in sight. Nor will we argue here the question whether there were not available alternative measures which might have eliminated the transfer difficulties.[1] From our point of view the answer is unsatisfactory, not for historical but for analytical reasons. As a description of what actually happened, or may happen, in a week of crisis it may or may not be accurate. But it does not go deep enough. It does not tell us why it is that transfer difficulties in this form should ever come to exist. It does not tell us why the business of settling payments between different places in different national areas should be associated with such difficulties.

This insistence on a more fundamental explanation may appear to be uncalled for. We are so

[1] I have outlined an analysis of these problems in chaps. v. and vi. of my *Great Depression*.

used to apprehensions concerning the balance of trade between different countries that to ask why they should exist may appear to be questioning the obvious. But a little reflection should show that this is not so. If by an effort of imagination we can discard our nationalistic blinkers, it is clear enough that there does exist a problem. There is nothing in political boundaries as such —as distinct from the policies pursued within them—which would justify us in taking it for granted that purchases across the boundaries of a sovereign state have a significance fundamentally different from purchases across the boundary of a local government area. We know that the prosperity of different *counties* in the same country often varies as widely as the prosperity of different *countries* in different parts of the world. Yet when South Wales is depressed there is no " problem " of monetary transfer to London. When Australia is depressed there is. There is surely a puzzle here which lies deeper than the gossip of the exchange market. Why do we have stability and an absence of friction in the one case, instability and difficulty in the other?

It is certainly not because of differences in the mobility of labour. The classical economists distinguished international from domestic trade on the ground that within national political areas labour was free to move from one industry to another, whereas between them it was not. This may or may not have been sensible for their particular purposes.[1] But it has no relevance to the problem of monetary transfer. Labour may be more mobile between London and South Wales than between London and Sydney. But it is not so mobile as to equalize out any differences of prosperity within the period in which monetary transfer has to be made. Yet there has been no "breakdown" of the exchanges with South Wales and there has been with Australia.

It is often suggested that the difference is due to tariffs. Countries are surrounded by tariffs. Counties are not. At first sight this is more plausible. Tariffs do render more difficult the business of exchange. If they are suddenly raised, they necessitate readjustments of prices and incomes which, in countries with independent banking systems, may be very hard to bring about. But this does not really go to the root of the matter. It is impossible to believe that the existence of tariffs as such is the condition for the existence of a transfer "problem". So long as the present internal banking structure persisted, it does not seem as if the erection of even high local *octrois* against the produce of

[1] In fact this assumption enabled the classical economists to construct a theory of value in a regime of non-competing groups, which had more generality than their main theory. It is clear that the identification of national areas with the concept of non-competing groups did not add to the analytical significance of the theory thus elaborated. And it is doubtful whether empirically the identification was justified.

T

South Wales would create inter-local monetary difficulties—any more than the raising of local costs of transport. The depression in South Wales and elsewhere (save in coalfields now protected against Welsh competition) would be greater. That is all.

Nor can we accept the view that it is the existence of different kinds of money which is, in itself, responsible for the difficulty. Where monies of different denomination exist, either side by side in the same area, or separately in different areas, undoubtedly there arises the necessity for money-changing arrangements. But this is not necessarily a very important complication. It is a nuisance rather than a " problem ". If the media of exchange in the different countries are composed of the same metal and if they are minted on demand and freely meltable and exportable, the fact that they are of different weights and fineness is a minor accident, incapable of giving rise to serious difficulties. If owing to changes in demand or supply the stream of purchases in one direction is greater than in the other, then there is simply a geographical redistribution of the precious metal of which the money is composed. The different coins or bars continue to exchange at rates determined by their respective weights and technical qualities.

If none of these theories is correct, it seems as if the only possible explanation of differences between local and national transfer must be the existence of differences of banking structure in different national areas. And in a sense this is true. The fact that, under twentieth-century conditions, within a common political area, there exists a single reserve banking structure, whereas between areas there are no reserves in common, does complicate the business of transfer considerably. Transfer from one branch to another of a single bank involves an automatic offsetting of equal amounts of spending power. Transfer from one bank to another in a single reserve system is likely, though not certain, to have the same effect. But transfer from one reserve system to another may be accompanied by either net additions to or subtractions from the total volume of credit outstanding.

So much is frequently realized. And when it has been realized, the defenders of the view that there is something " natural ", something economically inevitable, in the difference between national and local transfer are apt to imagine that they have proved their point. In spite of the sophistications of shallow critics, such as David Hume, with his unhelpful sneers about the Heptarchy,[1] a *really subtle* economic

---

[1] " Did not long experience make people easy on this head, what a fund of gloomy reflections might calculations afford to a melancholy YORKSHIREMAN, while he computed and magnified the sums drawn to London by taxes, absentees, commodities, and found on comparison the opposite articles so much inferior ? And, no doubt, had the *Heptarchy*

analysis has vindicated the view that there is something different between counties and countries after all!

But really this is still all very superficial. If we did not know how deep-rooted are the nationalistic prepossessions of even the best of us, it would be almost unbelievable that any economist would be content to stop at this point. It is very well known that techniques are available whereby transfer between different reserve systems can be harmoniously adjusted. The position between reserve systems in different countries need not differ conspicuously from the position between different branch banking systems in the same country. The transfer " problem " only arises where the efficient working of such techniques is frustrated by other influences.

Now it is just here that the political division of the world into different sovereign states, each claiming the right to regulate the local currency and banking arrangements, is all-important. If the world had been united into one federal state, no doubt there would have still remained banking problems of great importance. But it is fairly safe to say that the " problem " of transfer and

subsisted in ENGLAND the legislature of each state had been continually alarmed by the fear of a wrong balance : and as it is probable that the mutual hatred of these states would have been extremely violent on account of their close neighbourhood, they would have loaded and oppressed all commerce, by a jealous and superfluous caution " (*Essays Moral, Political and Literary* (ed. Green and Grose), vol. i. p. 335).

interlocal equilibrium in the form in which we know it would not be one of them.

This political factor has operated in a number of ways. In the first place, since banks in different states are subject to different laws, it has at once limited the spread of banking institutions which transcend frontiers and it has fostered the growth of national reserve systems. Whether the ideal banking structure is composed of many independent reserve banks or of one central reserve system, it is surely obvious that, if it had not been for the political factor, the existing organization of banking would have been radically different. There would have been a much greater spread of branch banking across the state frontiers. Whatever the arrangements for last-resort lending, there would certainly not have been a reserve bank in every area claiming political sovereignty. The business of international clearing would be organized on lines which made political frontiers irrelevant.

But this is not all. The political factor acts positively as well as negatively. When the area of the local reserve system runs parallel with the area of political sovereignty, there is great danger that, when strain arises, the authorities of the system will be prevented from taking the action which is necessary if equilibrium is to be preserved. They can be prevented from allowing local credit to contract or—what in a progressive society is more probable—from restraining it from expanding as rapidly as elsewhere. *The area of strain will be coterminous with the area of administrative discretion.* And the probability is that this discretion will be exercised.

We can see this perhaps most vividly if we revert to our Welsh example. Fortunately for the stability of economic life within the United Kingdom, South Wales is part of a unified area. When therefore the state of the balance of trade between South Wales and the rest of the country implies a diminution of spending power in South Wales, the process is quite automatic. Deposits in South Wales run down. Deposits elsewhere increase. In existing conditions, this takes place whether the banks in South Wales are branches of the larger system or not. There may be bankruptcies in South Wales. If there were local banks, some of them might go under. But the people would go on settling their business in pounds sterling. If there were a real " shortage " of pounds it would pay other banks to make the necessary arrangements. Of a permanent transfer difficulty, or a permanent difference between the value of a pound in South Wales and elsewhere, there would be no question.

But consider what would almost certainly have been the case if South Wales had been an independent sovereign state with a separate central bank under the control of the government treasury.

INTERNATIONAL MONEY

As conditions in South Wales worsened, we should have begun to hear of strain on the Welsh exchanges. The central bank would almost certainly have been prevented from taking the measures necessary to keep its reserve intact and the exchange in step with London. The shrewder and more far-sighted inhabitants of South Wales would guess that a break was likely and, wishing to save their capital, would withdraw money to hoard it or to keep it in London. They would be denounced as lacking in feeling for the land of their fathers. But the drain would continue. There would be a crisis in which the gold standard would be suspended, after which there would supervene a period of rigid exchange control (and consequent worsening of conditions generally), export subsidies to Welsh coal, etc., or fluctuating Welsh exchanges. Hordes of " experts " would travel down to Cardiff to diagnose the cause of the disaster and write books about it. They would attribute it to every possible circumstance save the one obviously responsible : the inability of a banking system subject to political pressure to take steps to keep in equilibrium.

In the last analysis, therefore, it is the political factor which gives rise to the economic problem of international monetary transfer. If historical accident had not created independent sovereign states, with independent claims to control the unit in which debts are settled and the policy of local banks, no such " problem " would have arisen. In a world state with a world money, there might be severe financial difficulties in particular areas. Local banks might over-lend and go bankrupt. Local producers might suffer such a curtailment of demand for their products that they were unable to pay their debts to creditors in other parts of the world. But there would be no abandonment of the international standard, no breakup of the international monetary unity. The thing simply could not happen if it were not for the intervention of independent sovereign states.

3. But is this good or bad ? Is it conducive to the most effective territorial division of labour that local governments should possess this power of initiative ? It is doubtful whether any advocate of the regime of monetary nationalism has ever gone so far as to claim that it is better that the world should be thus divided, that if independent sovereignty did not exist, then in the interest of monetary policy it would be desirable to invent it. But arguments are frequently used which do definitely imply as much. We must not take it for granted that the existence of monetary arrangements, which vary according to the area of sovereignty and which involve differences between international and interlocal transfer, will necessarily be regarded as undesirable. At the present day the policy of international money

and fixed exchanges has many powerful opponents. Before we enquire further into the way in which national systems are likely to work in practice, it is desirable to examine their objections.

It is probably the most frequent objection to a regime of international money that, in changing conditions, it involves changes in the relative quantities of money available in different parts of the system. If the demand for the products of, say, the Argentine falls off and the demand for the products of Australia increases, then there will be a relative decrease in the quantity of money in the Argentine and a relative increase in the quantity of money in Australia. Unless this happens, then sooner or later, if the change in demand is permanent, transfer difficulties will arise. But this is abhorrent to the exponents of monetary nationalism. "Never," they say with indignation, "never should the maintenance of international equilibrium be permitted to inflict deflation on the local economy. Never should we sacrifice our industries to this fetish of gold parities."

All this sounds very impressive. But if we look into it a little its plausibility seems to diminish. "Never, when we make more payments to our creditors than our creditors make to us, must our balances be allowed to diminish." This is the same proposition couched in less question-begging terms. To use the term deflation, not only to describe net contraction in the system as a whole, but also to describe these shifts of purchasing power within the system, is to confuse the issue in a manner which can only have propagandist justification. Deflation in the system as a whole is a senseless thing. It is an actively disequilibrating tendency. It is most improbable that any reputable economist would be found to give it active support. But a contraction of money incomes in some lines of production, reflecting a change of demand for the factors of production there, in favour of factors of production elsewhere for whose products demand has expanded, is not disequilibrating. So far from being disequilibrating, it is a change which may be absolutely necessary if equilibrium is to be preserved. Very often, if the money supply as a whole is increasing and the change of demand is not great, an absolute contraction of money incomes is not necessary. It is only necessary that money incomes elsewhere should increase more rapidly. But to demand that this should always be the case, to demand that the money supply should increase so rapidly that money incomes never anywhere needed adjustment downwards, would be to demand fairly rapid inflation in the system as a whole. Unless the mobility of factors of production were to become equal to the mobility of demand—which in the case of land and fixed capital is impossible and in the case of labour highly improbable—some money incomes must sometimes be adjusted in a downward direction. But to use the term deflation, with all its associations of general disequilibrium, to describe these necessary shifts, is either to misunderstand or deliberately to misrepresent the nature of the process involved. When the demand for cotton piece goods diminishes and the demand for silk increases, it is not really very helpful to speak of deflation in the cotton industry and inflation in the silk industry.

Of course, it is quite possible that a shift of demand from the products of local industry may bring about changes in relative preferences for liquid balances and other assets, which may involve, for the time being, a downward fluctuation of incomes which is more than that involved by the original shift of demand. But, even so, before we decide that deflation has taken place, or is likely to take place, in the system as a whole, we must look to what is happening in those other parts of the system to which demand is transferred. It is possible that there may be net deflation. But it is equally possible that there may be net inflation. Much depends on the general state of trade. But in any case, if such disequilibrating tendencies do arise, it is surely reasonable to demand that they should be dealt with internationally—not that the monetary unity of the world should be violently disrupted or permanently destroyed. We never dream of dealing with such difficulties by exchange fluctuations when they do not coincide with areas of political independence. We should not proceed to cut loose the Lancashire exchanges if the demand for cotton were to diminish.

But now we must take account of a more formidable argument. The more consistent advocates of monetary nationalism would not deny the necessity of changes in relative incomes in different industries and different places if there are relative changes of demand for the products of local factors of production. But in the modern world, they urge, these adjustments are not allowed to take place. Money incomes, especially money wages, are rigid, and if there is an adverse shift of demand for the products of a national area, or if, for some other reason, change is necessary, the impact of the change exhausts itself in producing unemployment and further depression. It is to circumvent this, they argue, that independent national monies are necessary. If the currencies in different areas are not linked by being based on a common metal, then, as demand shifts, the rate of exchange will fluctuate and so bring about the necessary changes in relative real incomes *via* changes in relative prices rather than *via* changes in money incomes. The fluctuating exchange and the independent national currency are devices for getting round the rigidity of money incomes.

Now there can be no doubt that the rigidity of money incomes is a great obstacle to the smooth working of the forces of the market. It is one of the great problems of our time. In part it is due to the existence of various governmental policies which are anti-liberal in character—the limitation of movement, the granting of special privileges to trade unions, forms of unemployment relief which are administered without regard to their effect on the market. Yet even under purely liberal institutions a downward adjustment of wages would be a slower and more difficult process than a fluctuation of the exchange. In any case, it would be an advantage if the same result could be achieved in an easier way.

But it is really very naïve to suppose that this is likely to happen. From the humanitarian point of view, it seems very attractive to substitute the automatic fluctuations of the exchange market for the tedious adjustments of the market for personal services. And, no doubt, once or twice in a century, in time of great crisis, it may be possible to do it. But to assume that it can become the normal means of adjusting real wages is to assume that the wage-earners are completely devoid of powers of observation and—what is even more difficult to believe, to judge by their present behaviour—that the experts and the politicians who plan these beneficent little tricks are completely silent in public about their intentions, both before and after the event. And this is really a most absurd assumption. Sooner or later the wage-earners, or their representatives, will perceive what is happening and will demand increased money wages to offset the rise in import prices. If they will not accept the view that changes in the value of their product necessitate changes in the remuneration of their services in money terms, it is futile to suppose that they will be so blind as to accept without struggle the view that they involve changes in their real incomes. The belief that wage-earners are concerned only with money incomes may afford a pretext for amusing theoretical fantasy. But—fortunately or unfortunately—it does not happen to be correct. After recent events in France, it does not even seem plausible.

But let us assume, for the purposes of argument, that it is. Let us assume that, so far as the wage-earners are concerned, the mechanism works as planned. No attempt is made to evade the effects on real incomes of the fluctuation of the external value of the national money. Even so, it is a complete and a pathetic delusion to suppose that in every other respect the system would work as if there were a common money.

It would not be the same as regards day-to-day trade. The risk would be very much greater.

Even where there existed a satisfactory market in forward exchange, there would still be a risk to be paid for that would be absent under a common currency. And, as recent experience has demonstrated, there are severe limits to what may be expected of a market in forward exchange.

It would not be the same as regards investment. Even under the most favourable circumstances the volume of international investment must shrink, if there are fluctuations in the relative value of the money in which revenue is earned and the money in which interest or dividends are paid. Even such comparatively small fluctuations as the fluctuations of the silver exchanges have restricted international investment. The fluctuations in a world of independent national monies would restrict it still more.

But all this is still to assume that the mechanism works as postulated. It is to assume that, in a world of independent currencies, the fluctuations of the free exchanges will have an equilibrating tendency. It is just this assumption which it is necessary to challenge directly. For there is no reason to believe that it is in any way justified. On the contrary both theory and experience suggest that, in a world in which exchange disequilibrium has become general, the fluctuations of the exchanges have an actively disequilibrating tendency. So far from bringing about a state of affairs in which equilibrium is reached more quickly than under a common international money, they bring about a state of affairs in which there is no reason to suppose that equilibrium will arrive at all. Even assuming that they do not give rise to a multitude of trade restrictions and controls of financial transactions —and of course it is notorious that this is perhaps their most conspicuous influence—they tend to cause deflation in some price structures, inflation in others and such a general upset of the liquidity preferences of the public in general, that, while they persist, there is cumulative financial chaos. Anything more unlike the expectations of the amiable exponents of general monetary nationalism it is scarcely possible to imagine.

The reason for the mistake is obvious. The purchasing power parity theory of the foreign exchanges asserts that the external value of money tends to reflect the relation between internal and external prices. This is true enough, and properly interpreted it is fundamental. It is also true that, if a small state lets go its exchange *in a world which is otherwise stable*, the fluctuation of that exchange will come to rest about a point which might be predicted from an inspection of internal and external price levels before the event takes place. There are many examples in history of small raw material producing areas which have succeeded in getting nearer to equilibrium by measures of this kind. But to assume that a

INTERNATIONAL MONEY

similar effect will follow, *if exchange fluctuations become general*, is completely to beg the question. For it assumes that the fluctuations of the exchanges will have no effect on prices, and this is not likely to be the case. When the important exchanges fluctuate, the commodity markets are shaken. The internal prices, between which the free exchange is to bring about equilibrium, are themselves disturbed. The free exchanges become an active disturbing influence. And there seems no reason at all to suppose any necessary tendency to equilibrium. It is just a vicious circle of inflation or deflation.

In such circumstances, in the absence of further intervention on the part of the different national governments, the self-interest of the different citizens would lead to a solution once more conducive to equilibrium. Either they would choose, from the welter of unstable currencies, that which seemed the least unstable, and settle their transactions in that; or they would turn to some new medium of exchange—bar gold, for example—whose value seemed relatively immune from the vagaries of governments, and make that their money. The intense inconvenience of a multiplicity of national monies would provide a powerful incentive to the reconstitution of a common international money.

But of course such behaviour would conflict completely with the central aims of the policy of monetary nationalism. That the citizens of the national area should be able to defeat the policy of their own state by using some other money, or by keeping their resources in bar gold, must necessarily be regarded as intolerable from the nationalist point of view. Hence contracts in terms other than the national currency will be held null and void. The holding of currencies other than the national currency or the hoarding of the precious metals will be prohibited. Foreign exchange acquired in any way will be confiscated with or without compensation. Citizens may even be threatened with death for not using the national money—as in Nazi Germany. In short, a complete regime of exchange controls and control of foreign trade must be instituted—with the results we have already analysed. There are many kinds of economic nationalism which lead to the isolation of the national economy by slow and almost imperceptible degrees. But monetary nationalism is not so dilatory. There is no form of nationalism more swiftly effective to disrupt the world economy than nationalism in the sphere of money. Of all forms of economic nationalism, monetary nationalism is the worst.

4. It is probable that this conclusion would be extensively recognized nowadays. The experience of the last few years has not been favourable to the cause of monetary nationalism. The forma-

tion of the sterling club, immediately the period of instability began, was in itself an acknowledgment of the dangers of a regime of free exchanges. The conditions of the various areas constituting the sterling club were so different that by no stretch of imagination could the arrangements thus made be justified by the standard arguments for areas of free exchange. There was no homogeneity of cost levels in the sterling area which could possibly afford a justification for fluctuating sterling exchanges *vis-à-vis* the rest of the world. The obvious justification for the arrangement was that, within the area, there was exchange stability. Sterling was not an international money. But it was an approach to an international money. In so far as the sterling club was to be justified at all, it was to be justified in these terms.

Moreover, the state of affairs prevailing as between the rival systems, the pound, the dollar and the gold currencies, was such as to justify the worst apprehensions of the theory of free exchanges. Trade was reduced. Long-term investment was negligible. There was extreme deflation in the weaker areas. Obstacles to trade of all kinds multiplied to a degree unprecedented in past history. Whether the crisis of 1931 was inevitable or whether by appropriate policy it could have been avoided, is a question on which reasonable men may well differ. But on the effects on trade and investment and on the shattering repercussions on international politics of the exchange uncertainties which succeeded it, there cannot be two opinions.[1]

But monetary nationalism dies hard. It is no longer believed that all will be for the best in the best of all possible worlds if each national currency is left perfectly free to find its own level. It is realized that when the great currencies are adrift there is no necessary level for each of them to find. It is realized that, in the absence of international money, the international economy disintegrates. The disadvantages, even of gold, are less emphasized, its advantages increasingly acknowledged. But it is still thought that within the framework of an international system the local rates of exchange should be adjustable. By all means let each nation link up to gold once more, it is said. But let them reserve their freedom to vary the rate of exchange if necessity arises. In this way we shall have the advantages

---

[1] Suppose that early in 1932, after the first convulsions of the crisis were over, Great Britain had returned to gold at perhaps 4 dollars to the pound. We should probably have had to pay more for conversion. But it is doubtful whether the dollar would have been devalued. We might have saved the Brüning regime in Germany. The period of deflation in the Gold Bloc countries might have been avoided. And the rate of exchange would have been more favourable to the surmounting of the rigidities of the British cost structure than it is likely to be again. It is not very profitable to prolong such conjectures. But I do not think that, in the verdict of history, those who urged such a policy and who consistently predicted the political convulsions ahead if it were not adopted will be written down as such fools as they were generally represented to be at the time.

of both systems, the stability of gold and the flexibility of paper.

Now there is no dispute that, after a period of extreme monetary nationalism, the return to a system of completely international money must necessarily be gradual. In reconstituting the international standard, it would not be prudent to fix once and for all rates of exchange which might prove to necessitate extensive local contraction or expansion in order to be immediately workable. Once an international system is in being, it is desirable that the appropriate local expansions and contractions should be made. If they are made at once they seldom need to be large. But while it is coming into being it is wise to avoid imposing big changes. Quite apart from the disturbance they cause, they are likely to discredit the idea of international money as such. The monetary authorities of the world are not ill-advised to guard against a repetition of the errors of 1925.

But it is one thing to leave a certain margin within which rates may be varied during a period of provisional stabilization. It is another thing to elevate such an expedient to the status of permanent machinery. For if the rates of exchange between different national areas are variable beyond the limits created by the costs of transfer, then international money does not exist. We are still in a world of monetary nationalism.

We are still in a world in which the accident of political separation creates economic phenomena which would never arise in a unified monetary system. Trade is uncertain. International investment is limited. The development of financial institutions is distorted by arbitrary and irrelevant political limitations. The national standard may be more respectable when it is printed on gold. But if the denomination of the note can be varied without varying its gold content, it is still to all intents and purposes a paper standard. It is still an independent national money.

It is sometimes said that at the present day it is necessary to retain the elasticity of such standards on account of the danger of large transfers of short-term capital. A completely international standard worked well enough in the days when the international short-loan fund was small, it is said. The resources of the different national systems, wisely managed, were equal to the strain of any transfer; and the advantages of a common standard outweighed the disadvantages of any small adjustments which this necessitated. But in the post-war world it is different. Vast masses of short-term funds accumulate in the various centres and at a moment's notice they are prepared to migrate, like some scourge of God, spreading havoc and devastation in their wake. No international system can stand such convulsions. It is to guard against dangers such as these that the different nations must reserve their financial freedom.

Such an argument sounds highly professional. And to the lay public, to most of whom the mere existence of floating balances is only slightly less mysterious than the doctrine of the Real Presence, it seems utterly and completely convincing. All praise to the experts who identified these sinister influences. " Foreign devils " were at the bottom of all our troubles after all!

But in fact it rests upon a most singular confusion. It is quite true that the monetary history of recent times has been marked by the existence of abnormally large volumes of short-term money menacingly idle in the great financial centres of the world. It is true that the migration of these funds has created grave financial disturbances. But to regard these movements as being the cause of all the trouble is completely to put the cart before the horse. So far from being a cause in this sense, they are essentially a consequence, a consequence of the fundamental instability of expectations in a regime of monetary nationalism. The fact that they, too, cause further instability is important. But it should not blind us to their ultimate origin. Why is it that there are not these vast and sudden migrations of capital *within* the different national areas? Obviously because there is no apprehension that the different units of currency within the area will not exchange at par. Why is it that they do take place *between* the national areas ? Obviously because under monetary nationalism the possibility of change is very real and evident. So long as there exists the possibility of alterations of the rate of exchange, so long is there definitely created a situation in which prudent men will seek to avoid loss and adventurous men will seek to find profit. The disproportionate size and distribution of the international short loan fund in recent years is the way in which the capital supply has responded to the expectation of changes in local standards. And so long as this expectation is justified by arrangements which avowedly protect local autonomy in this respect, so long will this evil and other similar consequences of monetary nationalism continue. To perpetuate exchange instability in order to cure the evils which the expectation of exchange instability has brought about is not really very sensible.

It is sometimes thought that all these difficulties can be obviated if only the changes in local exchange rates are brought about by international agreement. Monetary nationalism is to be made respectable by being brought into a sort of monetary league of nations—a confederation, a *Staatenbund*, in which each state retains its own liberty to do anything it pleases but agrees to meet and discuss the conflicts of aims which this liberty inevitably generates. When the balance of trade of any area with the rest of the world becomes unfavourable, international agreement is to permit a downward movement of its exchanges.

Now no one will deny the desirability of international co-operation to restore a common international standard. The recent agreements between the United States, France and Great Britain have everywhere been hailed as a first step towards recovery. If changes in exchange rates were always the result of international agreement, the disturbance resulting therefrom would be considerably diminished.

But it is still open to question whether such arrangements are either possible or desirable as a permanent equilibrating mechanism. We may take it as almost certain that there will seldom be a proposal to move the gold parity of any local currency upwards: the tendency will usually be in the reverse direction. But putting this on one side, we may still question whether such revisions will be easy to arrange or whether they will be unaccompanied by harmful disturbances.

Let us consider the matter in rather more detail. In order that such adjustments may be effective, it is necessary that they should be continuous. A disequilibrium which could be remedied by a small adjustment at the beginning may need a much greater change if it is to be remedied later on. But it is just at such a point that the claim for readjustment will be least plausible. The representatives of the national areas whose exports will suffer if the change is made will not be likely to be impressed by the plea for the correction of a small evil. They will urge delay and the adoption of other measures. They will ask why they should submit to disturbance to remedy the results of the wrong policies of others. But, if delay takes place and other measures are not adopted, the disequilibrium will be aggravated. Political strain will develop. Rumours of great struggles in the arena of state treasuries will be rife. There will develop all the secondary consequences of expected change which are agreed to be so damaging. The business of the world will be embarrassed while the politicians dispute. In the end, in the absence of a federal overriding power, one or other of the contesting parties may quite likely " assert its freedom " with consequences with which the events of the last few years have made us very familiar. Mr. Keynes has said that the Council of the Bank for International Settlements who contemplate a return to a regime of fixed gold parities " are living in . . . a fools' world ".[1] But what shall we say of the state of mind of those who conceive the function of a Bank which was set up to facilitate the smooth working of international money to consist in the arrange-

[1] *Lloyds Bank Review*, October 1925, p. 532.

ment of compromises between the policies of monetary nationalism?

The fact is that the whole conception is essentially *political* in character. If there were no sovereign states, no tradition that the alteration of the value of money was the sovereign's inalienable prerogative, the idea of adjustable parities would not occur to anyone. Who would suggest, if sovereignty were not divided, that the main function of a world clearing bank was to change the rates at which it transferred deposits from one account to another? The idea would be regarded as fantastic. And, from the point of view of international liberalism, any suggestion that, in a world that falls short of complete federation, similar arrangements would not have similarly wasteful and disequilibrating effects must be regarded as fantastic too. It is not merely fantastic. It is reactionary. It seeks to perpetuate a state of affairs which lead not towards international unification but away from it. It tends to perpetuate the conditions of the rampant nationalism which is destroying the civilization of Europe.

5. If this is correct, it seems as if there is no argument which would lead us to abandon the presumption that, in an international economy, an international money is desirable. In the liberal world federation, the law relating to

money would be a federal, not a state, function. And, whatever the general policy directing this law, it would not break up the unity of the world by the provision of separate local currencies with exchange rates fluctuating between the different areas.

This conclusion applies too to a world which falls far short of general federation. What the world needs to-day is an international money immune from the meddling of national governments—a Maria Theresa dollar up to date, which passes as currency in the different national areas. In recent years, so great has been the intrusion of national governments, that this function has come to be discharged by bar gold. But this is retrogressive. We do not need to go back to a currency which must be valued by weight rather than by tale. What is needed rather, after a due period of provisional stabilization, is that the relation of the different currencies to gold shall be fixed and then left alone. If any permanent international agreement is to take place it should take the form of an undertaking by the national states to allow the use of each other's currency throughout the whole of their respective areas and to enforce contracts in whatever unit they are made. Short of world federation in the sense we have indicated, this would be the best safeguard against a recrudescence of monetary nationalism. At the first sign of relative depreciation of the local currency all transactions would be effected in other money. But unless sovereignty itself is surrendered, the danger must always be great that such undertakings will be broken.[1]

6. But there still remains the problem of banking policy. The nineteenth century, which witnessed such considerable progress towards international currency unity, witnessed too the development of banking institutions which have provided the instruments for policies inimical to that unity. Whether or not central banking, in some form or other, would have arisen spontaneously is a difficult question, to which reasonable men may well give different answers. But it is unquestionable that the actual development of central banks has been conditioned throughout by influences which have been essentially political. They have been set up to provide loans for governments ; and they have usually been maintained and supported against competition for reasons of a similar nature. There are few central banks with a history of any length which, at one time or other, have not been used as instruments for deliberate inflation. And, as Bagehot argued, even when they have not been used for political purposes, their peculiar position within the system

---

[1] See Richard Strigl, " Gibt es eine Sicherung gegen Inflation ", *Mitteilungen des Verbandes österreichischer Banken und Bankiers*, 1932, N. 15/6.

of national banking has made them a source of weakness in the system of international financial relations. And when governments have been inclined to use them as instruments of positive policy, they have become the most potent cause of general economic nationalism. If the government of a certain area imposes upon the banks under its jurisdiction a policy of expansion at a time when the local position offers no scope for such expansion, then, as we have seen, the international equilibrium is ruptured. The " problem " of maintaining international equilibrium at once arises—and with it all the policies designed to solve such a " problem ".

This clearly is the position of the world today. The majority of the central banks are being asked to serve two masters. They are being asked to maintain equilibrium between their system and the rest of the world and they are being asked to promote the aims of local economic policy—rearmament, public works, cheap credits to agriculture, and so on. Hence exchange controls, fluctuating exchanges, bilateral clearing, control of foreign investment, and all the other measures whose effects we have already examined.

In such a situation, it is tempting to argue that the logical solution is a complete unification of the various national systems through an international central bank. But against this there are powerful arguments. The case for the single reserve system is usually taken for granted as regards national areas; although it has certainly never been systematically demonstrated from any other than a nationalistic point of view, and although many of the best minds (including Walter Bagehot, the leading exponent of the principles of central banking) have expressed grave doubts as to its validity.[1] But the case for a single reserve system for the world is certainly not generally conceded: and though most of the arguments against it are nationalistic in character, there are others which are by no means of this order. A single reserve system directly under the pressure of an international government would run grave danger of being used for inflationary purposes. It is doubtful whether it would provide so rapid a response to local changes in the investment situation as less centralized institutions. Nor has it yet been shown that a multi-reserve system, in which each institution was completely unprotected by the state and completely liable to the strict application of the law of bankruptcy, would produce fluctuations of the money supply more conducive to disequilibrium than a single reserve system subject to political pressure.

The truth is that, if we are honest, we must confess that at the present time our knowledge

---

[1] On all these problems, discussion of which in recent years has been so meagre, Dr. Vera Smith's *Rationale of Central Banking* contains much useful information.

both of the desiderata and of the possible instruments of general monetary policy is so imperfect that, even within the context of the general liberal idea, it is not possible to speak with any certainty concerning the most desirable ultimate form of international banking institutions. We know that it is desirable that there should be an international money. We know that it is desirable, therefore, that whatever the general policy adopted, the movements of cash and credit in the different parts of the system should preserve international equilibrium. But, although we know many things to avoid, we still dispute concerning what is to be regarded as the best general policy and we still dispute concerning the ultimately best institutions for realizing the aims of this policy.

But, for all this, the main requirement of immediate policy is fairly obvious. It may not yet be clear whether a single or a multiple reserve system is ultimately the best way to realize the aims of international liberalism. But it is clear, if these aims are to be realized, that control of *local* policy should be removed as far as possible from the influence of *local* governments; that, whatever their ultimate destiny, the different reserve systems should cease to be the instruments of monetary nationalism. The banking policy of the twenties, which sought to remove the central banks from the influence of governments, was right. The banking policy of the thirties, which has been to bring them once more under government control, is wrong. The immediate objective of policy, therefore, must be to reverse this tendency. In a world free from monetary nationalism, the solution of the remaining problems of banking policy should not present insurmountable difficulties.

CONCLUSION

CHAPTER XI

NATIONALISM OR INTERNATIONALISM

1. WE now reach the conclusion of our investigations. The last three chapters have been devoted to the discussion of different types of complete international planning. It has been argued that communism on an international scale must develop internal weaknesses which frustrate the achievement of its aims. But it has been argued, too, that liberalism exhibits none of these weaknesses and that an international liberal plan is conceivable which is technically workable and which is free from the manifest contradictions of other forms of planning.

But do we want an international system? Are there reasons why the organization of social life in national units offers advantages and attractions to the members of such units, sufficient to outweigh the advantages and attractions of the more comprehensive organization? Do national interests clash with the interests of the world as a whole? At the present day the tendency to national separatism is perhaps stronger than at any time in human history. On what grounds of utility or of idealism can such an attitude ultimately rest ?

It is to the examination of this question that our concluding chapter must be devoted.

2. We may take it as axiomatic that, on the assumption that war is to be a permanent instrument of national policy, there are reasons which may justify for particular national groups some interference with the maximum international division of labour. Defence may be much more important than opulence. Arrangements which secure the continuous provision of materials or services essential to the conduct of war, even though they involve securing them at higher cost than would otherwise be necessary, are capable of justification on the grounds of this necessity. It is not certain that to foster home production is always the best method. Too much sacrifice of this sort may be less productive than direct expenditure on safeguarding lines of communication. But, on the assumption that security against attack is necessary, measures which produce it at the sacrifice of the other ingredients of real income are not to be regarded as irrational. The correct apologia for the extravagant petting in recent years of the British Iron and Steel Industries is not that thereby we are made richer than we should have been had we bought in the

CH. XI NATIONALISM OR INTERNATIONALISM 311

cheapest market and used our own resources for other purposes, but rather that, while the danger of war persists, we may be ill-advised to depend so much on foreign sources for the main supply of iron and steel products essential for war purposes.

But all this assumes that defence is necessary. It assumes, that is to say, the continuance of the political structure which makes the necessity of defence a possibility: the retention by the national states of the right to use war as an instrument of policy. If this right were surrendered, if the danger of war were removed by more efficient political arrangements, the argument for economic nationalism on these grounds would be destroyed too. Unless the right to make war is to be regarded as an end in itself, the need to prepare for war can never be an argument for the retention of the political arrangements (or lack of arrangements) which make it necessary.

3. Let us therefore abstract from this danger. Assuming that the danger of war could be removed by the supersession of independent state sovereignty by some kind of federation, let us enquire whether there may not be reasons of a more "economic" nature which should lead the members of the different national states to pursue policies of national separatism. Are there possibilities of national gain from restriction of the

international division of labour ? We are on very familiar ground here and our argument may move swiftly.

It is certainly quite possible to conceive of cases in which one national group may gain at the expense of others. The popular arguments for protection are, of course, almost wholly fallacious. To maintain an industry, as such, regardless of whether the factors of production thus employed are as productive there as they would be if devoted to other uses, is as fruitless from the point of view of the majority of the inhabitants of the national area as it is from the point of view of the majority of the inhabitants of the world as a whole. Nothing that has been said in earlier chapters concerning the waste of protecting particular groups of undertakings from the competition of undertakings able to meet demand at lower cost, ceases to be applicable when we turn from the international to the national economy. Protection to particular lines of industry protects, not the nation, but the industry. It is in the interests of the industry that the government shall act in this way. But so far as the rest of the nation are concerned their interests are directly frustrated. Even the celebrated argument for the protection of infant industries has worn a little thin by now. Analytically the thing is conceivable. But in fact it does not seem to happen. The infants are brought to birth. But they never cease to need protection.

CH. XI NATIONALISM OR INTERNATIONALISM 313

There is no reprieve for the "*the* industry" fallacy here.

But there are arguments for national restriction, either by tariffs or other forms of planning, which are not so obviously fallacious. We all know that, if the members of an industrial group restrict output below the competitive limit, it is quite conceivable, if their position is monopolistic, that their aggregate takings may be increased. We know too that if a group of buyers in a favourable strategic position restrict their purchases the price at which they can buy may fall so much that their profits are actually enhanced. Clearly the same possibilities are conceivable for the members of geographical groups. Indeed, as we have seen already, if the members of national groups are organized as trading monopolies there is the strongest probability that they will attempt to pursue these gains. Either by limiting sales or by reducing purchases, it is possible that they may turn the terms of trade in their favour. It is probable that the circumstances in which long-run gains of this sort are possible for the inhabitants of actual national areas are not very frequent. In the short run, the sources of supply or demand may be squeezable. But, in the long run, monopolistic advantage of this sort is much harder to retain. Yet the possibility exists and should be explicitly recognized.

This is not all. In addition to the possibility of using restriction to obtain long-run advantage in exchange, there is the possibility of using it for alleviating short-run disequilibrium of employment. To argue that the volume of employment is a function of the height of tariff walls is, of course, a crude fallacy. The percentage of unemployment has been as high in protectionist America and Germany as ever in free-trade England—indeed it has been considerably higher. But it remains true that when tariffs or other restrictions are first imposed they may avert a contraction of credit that would otherwise have been necessary, or may permit an expansion of credit that would otherwise have been impossible. Once these effects have exhausted themselves, the restrictions are no further aid to employment. The barriers must be raised once more if the same effect is to be repeated. But, at the moment that they are first erected, the effect on employment may be favourable.

These conclusions are well known. They are direct deductions from quite simple principles of analytical economics. But, before they can be made any justification for restrictionism as a national policy, it must be shown that the policy of other nations is unaffected. For the assumption that other things remain equal is quite essential to the validity of all these arguments. If the government of one nation attempts to turn the terms of trade in its favour by restrictionism and the policy of other nations remains unchanged, it is possible that it may be successful. But if the others take similar measures, then whatever happens to the terms of trade, it is much more probable that wealth will be spilt all round. Similarly if the government of one nation attempts to " cure unemployment " by tariffs or such like measures, and all the others remain quiescent, the internal credit expansion which this makes possible may have some transitory success. But if all nations simultaneously adopt such measures, the net effect is likely to be not reflationary but deflationary. Although some particular branches of industry may benefit, the general effect will be, not to increase employment, but to diminish it.

But it is just this possibility which is overwhelmingly likely. It is not in the least probable that the governments of the world will stand acquiescent while the governments of a single area conduct experiments based on the Marshall curves or the propositions of the *Treatise on Money*. All experience, all common sense, suggests the contrary. Rightly or wrongly, they will decide that what is sauce for the goose is sauce for the gander and, in the resulting competition of restrictionism each party is likely to suffer. Economists who in recent years have made a technical analysis which assumes other things to be equal, the basis of prescriptions as to policy in cases where other things are almost certain not to be equal, have done grave disservice. They may have gained some cheap repute with the unthinking crowd, anxious as usual for a cabalistic rationalization of its own prejudices. But they have given bad advice to the world : and they have brought the fine discipline of analytical economics into ridicule. It was not thus that the great men who discovered the methods of pure analysis conceived their application to practice.

In practice it is highly improbable that restriction of trade will secure permanent advantage to the majority of the national group.

4. The most plausible case for national restrictionism lies, not in the sphere of trade, but in the sphere of migration. The economic effects of changes in the working population of a national area are subtle and difficult to analyse, especially when account is taken of the important fact that the population is hardly ever homogeneous. It is certainly wrong to assert baldly that movement into an area must necessarily lower the incomes of the majority of the people already living in that area, or that movement out must necessarily always benefit those who remain. The former proposition could not possibly apply to the peopling of the American continent, nor the latter to emigration from Great Britain if the population

were already greatly reduced. The application to the fluctuations of a heterogeneous population of crude extensions of a law of diminishing returns which applies essentially to variations of homogeneous divisible factors obviously begs all the difficult questions raised by the existence of different classes of factors with different degrees of divisibility. The economics of migration are not as simple as all that. Most of the " economic " arguments in favour of limitation of either immigration or emigration of the past have been devised, not with a view to the protection of the interests of the national group as a whole or the majority of its members, but rather with a view to the protection of interests of particular groups —the restriction of immigration in the interests of particular groups of labour, the restriction of emigration in the interests of particular groups of landlords and property owners.

Nevertheless it is not impossible to conceive of cases where, by the limitation of immigration, the inhabitants of rich but relatively sparsely inhabited areas may secure to themselves gains which would not occur if movement in were not limited. It is not very likely that such movements would often actually depress real incomes, though even that is conceivable. But it is certainly possible that it might prevent real incomes rising so rapidly as otherwise would be the case. If we remember that movements of labour are almost always accompanied by movements of capital, we shall realize that even this is not likely to be so general as popular opinion would have us believe. But it is a possibility which cannot be ruled out. Certainly for one area to remain open when all others are closed may sometimes give rise to difficulty.

But even here we must beware of casting our analysis within too static a framework. In a world in which technical knowledge and the general conditions of demand are changing rapidly, conditions of free migration, which at one time seem to involve disadvantage to the inhabitants of particular areas, may at another time be conducive to their advantage. It may be advantageous to be able to exclude emigrants from areas for whose products demand has contracted. But it may also be advantageous to be able to migrate elsewhere when demand for one's own products diminishes. It may be natural to demand the one without being willing to concede the other. But it is hardly logical to do so. And it is not to be expected that the inhabitants of other areas will fail to notice the inconsistency As we have seen already, if a similar attitude is adopted by the inhabitants of each national area, instability in general is increased. There can be little doubt that, over long periods, most national groups would be better off if national limitations on migration were removed.

NATIONALISM OR INTERNATIONALISM

5. But let us cast our net a little wider. If war is not to be regarded as an ultimate good in itself, the avoidance of war is obviously a national interest. War destroys wealth. It destroys happiness. It destroys the subtle checks and controls which make civilized society possible. Under modern conditions even the cost of preparing for war bids fair to constitute a burden which will more than absorb all the fruits of technical progress.

It has sometimes been thought that this danger may be mitigated by a sacrifice of material well-being. If the various national states would organize their affairs on a basis of economic self-sufficiency, it is said, the dangers of war due to economic causes would be minimized. The inhabitants of each nation would be free to develop their own lives in their own way without the friction which comes from " economic entanglement " among nations. This was the view of the philosopher, Johann Gottlieb Fichte. It is the official apologia for the policy of contemporary Germany ; and, in our own less pretentious atmosphere, it has received the support of no less an authority than Mr. John Maynard Keynes.

" I sympathize," says Mr. Keynes, " with those who would minimize, rather than maximize, economic entanglement among nations. Ideas, knowledge, science, hospitality, travel—these are the things which should of their nature be international. But let goods be homespun wherever it is reasonably and conveniently possible . . . a greater measure of national self-sufficiency and economic isolation among countries than existed in 1914 may tend to serve the cause of peace rather than otherwise." [1]

The idea is plain. To secure peace, some sacrifice—Mr. Keynes thinks it need not be great—of the wealth which comes from international division of labour is desirable.

But unfortunately it seems to rest upon delusion. We will not pause to enquire how long " ideas, knowledge, science, hospitality, travel " are likely to remain free when goods are " as far as is reasonably and conveniently possible " homespun—though developments in those parts where such policies are now being applied scarcely seem to warrant much optimism here. But we must recognize that this policy is incapable of being generalized. Mr. Keynes, whose outlook in recent years sometimes appears disconcertingly insular, may be right in supposing that, within the Empire, it would be possible at some sacrifice to reach greater self-sufficiency than in the past, though there is reason to suppose that he greatly underestimates the sacrifice. There are certain other national groups in a similar position. But it is really ridiculous

[1] " National Self-Sufficiency ", *Yale Review*, vol. xxii. p. 758.

CH. XI NATIONALISM OR INTERNATIONALISM

to suppose that such a policy is possible for the majority, given their present national boundaries. Given the present political divisions of the world, to recommend autarky as a general policy is to recommend war as an instrument for making autarky possible.

No doubt Mr. Keynes would repudiate this. For, despite all the damage he has done to liberal policies in recent years, he is still the man who wrote the *Economic Consequences of the Peace*, one of the most magnificent gestures in defence of the great principles of peace and international justice of this or any other age. It would be absurd to depict Mr. Keynes in any way as a war-monger. But, if the analysis of these pages is correct, it is not absurd at all to depict war-mongering as the eventual consequence of the policies which, in a fit of premature discouragement at the absence of quick success of his earlier internationalism, he has been led, half desperately, half frivolously, to adopt. In all this he has been less logical than his predecessors. The philosopher Fichte, who recommended similar policies, saw more clearly on these matters.

"It has always been the privilege of philosophers to sigh over wars", wrote this rather prematurely *echt* Nordic type. "The present author does not love them more than anyone else. But he believes in their inevitability in the present circumstances and deems it uncalled for to complain of the inevitable. In order to abolish war, it is necessary to abolish its cause. Every state must receive what it intends to obtain by war and what *it alone* [our italics] can reasonably determine, that is its natural frontiers. When that is accomplished it will have no further claims on any other state since it will possess what it had sought." [1]

In fact the danger is even greater than this. For even if it were physically possible for the different national states to attain self-sufficiency at *some* level of real income, it is quite out of the question that they should attain it at the *same* level. So long as the inhabitants of the different states were prevented from bettering their position by exchange or by migration, some self-sufficient states would be richer than others. It would always be possible to hope that things would be improved by a forcible enlargement of frontiers. The populations of the East will be increasing long after the population of the West has become stationary or declining. If they are forcibly prevented from foreign trade, they are not likely to forget that, at no very distant date in the past, it was deemed justifiable to break down similar prohibitions on their part with

[1] *Der geschlossene Handelsstaat* (Tübingen, 1800), p. 218. I take the translation from the recent Richard Cobden lecture of Professor Rappard, *The Common Menace of Economic and Military Armaments*, a store of much wisdom and information on these topics.

cannons and bayonets. Who can believe that it is possible, year in year out, for the inhabitants of the richer countries of the world to withdraw into economic self-sufficiency without raising up against themselves combinations of the poorer Powers which are truly fearful to contemplate ?

All this has a most profound bearing on the question of restriction of migration, which we were discussing in the last section. It is conceivable, as we saw, that there may be areas whose economic conditions are such that the present inhabitants and their descendants will be permanently better off if they retain a position of geographical monopoly. But this assumes that they are able to retain it, that they are able permanently to defy the desire of the inhabitants of the areas less richly endowed to improve their position by migration. And this is a very big assumption. It is a very big assumption indeed, in a world in which politics are dominated more and more by appeals to mass emotion, to suppose that any limitation of migration *that is not internationally enforced* can be permanently supported against the pressure of the poorer and more populous nations. For a time, political accident and judicious alliance may permit wide disparities to persist. But to believe that they are permanently possible is to lose all historical perspective. If only for this reason, the preservation of national rights to control migration is a most dubious national interest.

6. If these considerations are correct, it seems to follow that there is no long-run advantage for the members of the different national groups from the preservation of national sovereignty. There is no gain from trade, there is no gain of security which would not be better provided for by some form of international federation.

We are left, then, with the question whether there is not some inherent virtue in national separatism, as such, which justifies the retention of such arrangements. Is there perhaps some ultimate good in the national form of community which is worth risking all the wastes and dangers of nationalism to preserve ?

We must not dismiss this question as frivolous. In spite of the excesses of continental nationalism, we must recognize that love of country and devotion to the national good are not negligible virtues. Patriotism is not always the last refuge of a scoundrel. The cosmopolitan is not always an improvement on the provincial. A man must have something outside himself to which he can give devotion if he is to be fully human. The nationalist at least has that.

But it may still be questioned whether, at the present stage of history, devotion to the nation, as such, is a very fruitful form of emotion.

The feelings associated with patriotism which we regard as good in themselves are not inseparable from particular forms of political organization. To love the landscape of the Oxford meadows or the fine flexibility of the English tongue, it is not necessary to love the Oxfordshire County Council or the English Board of Education. The sentiment of public service may be best evoked by institutions which are most conducive to human good. To find the ultimate goods of life in particular forms of political machinery, regardless of the suitability of that machinery to promote human happiness, is surely a delusion—a confusion of ends and means, of mechanism and purpose.

But this is just our danger. In the days of the decay of the great historical religions, men have deified the idea of the nation. They have made devotion to particular political machines a fanatical idolatry. They have erected a mythology of the state, or the race, more ridiculous, more inconsistent, more cruel than the superstitions of ancient barbarism. And because there is more than one state, there is conflict among the idols. Nothing can be more certain than that if we can find no ideals more compelling than this much of what is best in human achievement hitherto must perish.

But is this really so difficult? Dostoievsky once said that if we try to love all humanity we shall only end by hating all humanity. No doubt this is profoundly true. But international liberalism does not bid us love humanity. It seeks only to persuade us that co-operation between the different members of humanity is advantageous for the furtherance of individual ends. In this respect, it is true, it is merely the plan of a mechanism more efficient than the world of independent nations. Yet nevertheless the idea of the way of living with which it is associated is something more than that. A society which preserves spontaneity and freedom, with its manifold play of mind on mind and its world-wide heritage of art and learning—this surely is a conception as congenial to the aspirations of men who are not spiritually sick as any nationalism which turns inwards. We may no longer be able to believe the metaphysics of the age of faith. But, despite the antics of guttersnipe racialism, we need not cease to do homage to the idea of that fellowship in which there is neither Jew nor Greek, bond nor free. The ideals of Athens still challenge the ideals of Sparta.

7. It has been the argument of this essay that, in our day, these ideals can only be sustained by far-reaching political changes. On a long view, the interests of men who do not love violence, as such, are not in conflict. But if the political organization is sectional, it may give rise to

optical delusions, behind which the forces of violence and monopoly may manœuvre. The root of our present difficulties is not some inherent tendency to economic catastrophe but a political structure which has outlived its utility. Not capitalism, which, rightly conditioned, is a safeguard of liberty and progress, but nationalism, which tends to poverty and conflict, is the cause of our present distresses. What the world needs is not the socialist revolution, which, on every reasonable computation of the probabilities, would only develop still further the contradictions of nationalist separation, but the liberal reforms which would create a framework within which these contradictions would not be permitted to emerge.

Nationalism is something which must be surpassed. There was probably never a moment in the history of the world when such a task seemed so difficult to accomplish. But it can be accomplished if our hearts and minds tell us that it is necessary; and it must be accomplished if all that we regard as most valuable is not to perish in the wreck of our common civilization.

SELECT BIBLIOGRAPHY

THE argument of this essay makes no pretence to originality. Hence it has not been thought necessary to give detailed references to the various sources of each particular proposition. But for those readers to whom the general mode of approach is unfamiliar the following works may afford further elucidations of particular aspects of the argument. It must not be thought that their authors would necessarily be in agreement with the total case here presented, or that the author of the present work wishes in every respect to be thought to accept their position.

On the general theory of international trade and international trade policy, Professor Haberler's *Theory of International Trade* is probably the best and most comprehensive statement. The long-awaited treatise by Professor Jacob Viner, now happily reported to be approaching completion, will no doubt also be a standard work on this subject.

On the problems of trade policy, Marshall's *Memorandum on the Fiscal Policy of International Trade* and Professor Pigou's *Protective and Preferential Import Duties* (London School of Economics Reprint) are classical statements. Professor Taussig's *Free Trade, the Tariff and Reciprocity* and Professor Haberler's *Liberale und planwirtschaftliche Handelspolitik* should also be consulted. There are two most valuable essays by Professor Viner in the recent publication of the joint committee of the Carnegie Endowment and the International Chamber of Commerce, *The Improvement of Commercial Relations between Nations*; and the chapters by Sir William Beveridge, Professor Plant and Dr. Hicks in *Tariffs, the Case Restated*, edited by Sir William Beveridge, will be found helpful on special problems.

On the general international aspects of attempts to realize socialism on a national scale, the literature is meagre. The views here developed owe much to the works of the late Professor Edwin Cannan, especially sundry articles in *The Economic Outlook* and *An Economist's Protest*. There is a brief but highly significant section on this subject in Professor von Mises's *Socialism: an Economic and Sociological Analysis*, which should also be consulted on the economics of general collectivism.

The history of earlier attempts at national planning may be consulted in Professor Heckscher's monumental treatise on *Mercantilism*. The classical liberal attitude is best judged, not from the cheap travesties which appear in certain histories of economic thought, but from the original works of its founders—Hume, Adam Smith and Bentham.

On the all-important question of the economic causes of war, Professor Staley's *War and the Private Investor* is at once the most systematic and thorough treatment of the historical aspects of the case. Mr. Hawtrey's *Economic Aspects of Sovereignty* is stimulating and suggestive on the consequences of political separatism. And it would be unjust not to mention in this connection Sir Norman Angell, whose various works, although not primarily addressed to professional economics, mark an epoch in the discussion of these problems. His latest work, *This Have and Have-not Business*, contains an admirable restatement of his fundamental position.

On the difficult sociological problems of national sentiment and economic interest, Professor Sulzbach's *Nationales Gemeinschaftsgefühl und wirtschaftliches Interesse* should be consulted. There is also a little-known work of Professor von Mises, *Nation, Staat und Wirtschaft*, on the politics and economics of the Great War, which contains many pregnant suggestions.

The effects of recent economic policy in the international sphere are faithfully recorded year by year in Professor Condliffe's *World Economic Survey*, published by the Financial Section of the League of Nations Secretariat.

Printed in Great Britain by R. & R. CLARK, LIMITED, *Edinburgh*

WORLD AFFAIRS: National and International Viewpoints
An Arno Press Collection

Angell, Norman. **The Great Illusion, 1933.** 1933.

Benes, Eduard. **Memoirs:** From Munich to New War and New Victory. 1954.

[Carrington, Charles Edmund] (Edmonds, Charles, pseud.) **A Subaltern's War.** 1930. New preface by Charles Edmund Carrington.

Cassel, Gustav. **Money and Foreign Exchange After 1914.** 1922.

Chambers, Frank P. **The War Behind the War, 1914-1918.** 1939.

Dedijer, Vladimir. **Tito.** 1953.

Dickinson, Edwin DeWitt. **The Equality of States in International Law.** 1920.

Douhet, Giulio. **The Command of the Air.** 1942.

Edib, Halidé. **Memoirs.** 1926.

Ferrero, Guglielmo. **The Principles of Power.** 1942.

Grew, Joseph C. **Ten Years in Japan.** 1944.

Hayden, Joseph Ralston. **The Philippines.** 1942.

Hudson, Manley O. **The Permanent Court of International Justice, 1920-1942.** 1943.

Huntington, Ellsworth. **Mainsprings of Civilization.** 1945.

Jacks, G. V. and R. O. Whyte. **Vanishing Lands:** A World Survey of Soil Erosion. 1939.

Mason, Edward S. **Controlling World Trade.** 1946.

Menon, V. P. **The Story of the Integration of the Indian States.** 1956.

Moore, Wilbert E. **Economic Demography of Eastern and Southern Europe.** 1945.

[Ohlin, Bertil]. **The Course and Phases of the World Economic Depression.** 1931.

Oliveira, A. Ramos. **Politics, Economics and Men of Modern Spain, 1808-1946.** 1946.

O'Sullivan, Donal. **The Irish Free State and Its Senate.** 1940.

Peffer, Nathaniel. **The White Man's Dilemma.** 1927.

Philby, H. St. John. **Sa'udi Arabia.** 1955.

Rappard, William E. **International Relations as Viewed From Geneva.** 1925.

Rauschning, Hermann. **The Revolution of Nihilism.** 1939.

Reshetar, John S., Jr. **The Ukrainian Revolution, 1917-1920.** 1952.

Richmond, Admiral Sir Herbert. **Sea Power in the Modern World.** 1934.

Robbins, Lionel. **Economic Planning and International Order.** 1937. New preface by Lionel Robbins.

Russell, Bertrand. **Bolshevism:** Practice and Theory. 1920.

Russell, Frank M. **Theories of International Relations.** 1936.

Schwarz, Solomon M. **The Jews in the Soviet Union.** 1951.

Siegfried, André. **Canada:** An International Power. [1947].

Souvarine, Boris. **Stalin.** 1939.

Spaulding, Oliver Lyman, Jr., Hoffman Nickerson, and John Womack Wright. **Warfare.** 1925.

Storrs, Sir Ronald. **Memoirs.** 1937.

Strausz-Hupé, Robert. **Geopolitics:** The Struggle for Space and Power. 1942.

Swinton, Sir Ernest D. **Eyewitness.** 1933.

Timasheff, Nicholas S. **The Great Retreat.** 1946.

Welles, Sumner. **Naboth's Vineyard:** The Dominican Republic, 1844-1924. 1928. Two volumes in one.

Whittlesey, Derwent. **The Earth and the State.** 1939.

Wilcox, Clair. **A Charter for World Trade.** 1949.